HOW TO OVERCOME CHILDHOOD TRAUMA

ELEVATE SELF-IMAGE, CONQUER EMOTIONAL NEGLECT AND CULTIVATE DEEPER CONNECTIONS IN RELATIONSHIPS

MELI CRUZ

© **Copyright 2023 - All rights reserved.**

The content contained within this book may not be reproduced, duplicated or transmitted without direct written permission from the author or the publisher.

Under no circumstances will any blame or legal responsibility be held against the publisher or author for any damages, reparation, or monetary loss due to the information contained within this book, either directly or indirectly.

Legal Notice:

This book is copyright-protected. It is only for personal use. You cannot amend, distribute, sell, use, quote or paraphrase any part of the content within this book without the consent of the author or publisher.

Disclaimer Notice:

Please note the information contained within this document is for educational and entertainment purposes only. All effort has been executed to present accurate, up-to-date, reliable, and complete information. No warranties of any kind are declared or implied. Readers acknowledge that the author is not engaged in rendering legal, financial, medical or professional advice. The content within this book has been derived from various sources. Please consult a licensed professional before attempting any techniques outlined in this book.

By reading this document, the reader agrees that under no circumstances is the author responsible for any direct or indirect losses incurred as a result of the use of the information contained within this document, including, but not limited to, errors, omissions, or inaccuracies.

CONTENTS

Introduction 5

1. Unpacking Childhood Trauma 11
2. The Healing Journey—Understanding and Accepting 29
3. Building a Strong Self-Image—Rediscovering Your Identity 45
4. Self-Love and Self-Care—Nurturing Your Body, Mind, and Soul 55
5. Setting Boundaries—Taking Control of Your Personal Space 67
6. Redefining Relationships—Building Healthy Interpersonal Connections 81
7. Overcoming Obstacles—Resilience in the Face of Setbacks 93
8. Maintaining Progress—Ensuring Sustainable Healing 103
9. Thriving After Trauma—Cultivating a Life of Joy and Fulfillment 113

Conclusion 121
Glossary 125
References 127

INTRODUCTION

Are intrusive thoughts, negative self-image, and difficulty trusting others keeping you from living a satisfactory life? Trauma feels like being stuck in a sinking sandpit when it's left to fester. It can influence every aspect of your adult life, making it difficult to separate yourself from past wounds. Early traumatization can cause major struggles with self-esteem and confidence, negatively impacting how you respond to situations outside your control. During traumatic events, your sense of safety and trust is threatened, making you feel like a puppet to pain when you should be empowered to claim power over your life. Feelings of insecurity and mistrust from negative experiences tend to be carried into each growth stage, resulting in an emotional battle within. Challenges with emotional regulation can look like having frequent outbursts due to hypersensitivity. Difficulties with emotional control can also resemble numbness and an inability to express feelings, both of which can make navigating adulthood painful. It's also possible to experience childhood trauma and not be completely aware of it. A common case of this is childhood emotional neglect (CEN), which is when a parent or guardian fails to meet a child's needs during the early periods of development. Affection, support, and attention are examples of unmet needs in CEN; these will be explored in the book's first chapter. Childhood trauma can make it hard to cope with strong emotions. It can cause you to settle for unhealthy relationships, become a people pleaser, or avoid sharing yourself with others, and depriving yourself of connection worsens the heavy feeling of trauma. But just as trauma is possible, so is your empowerment and healing.

I like to think I had a normal childhood. My parents were good, hardworking professionals; we attended church three to four times weekly. My mother worked as a registered nurse, and my father worked as a licensed social worker. Nothing about my childhood appeared harmful at all. I grew up thinking it was all good, but once I became an adult, I had one failed relationship after another. This pattern made me question how "normal" my upbringing was. I've been working through my trauma with a therapist for almost five years now, and even with the progress, I still have trouble maintaining strong relationships. One day, I came across an Instagram video by Brian Yang, where he said,

> *"Better communication is not going to save your relationship. If you have the same fight over and over, you do not have a communication problem; you have an unresolved childhood trauma problem. This is why most couples therapy does not work. They are only trying to chip away at the very top surface of this iceberg when over eighty percent of it is submerged under the surface, in our nervous system, in our subconscious. For example, one person might feel alone, unseen, and unheard; the other might feel suffocated, controlled, or criticized. One person cannot relax if a conflict is not resolved immediately; the other person cannot relax unless they avoid the conflict. You see, these emotional pains are familiar, and if you sit with it long enough, you'll see that*

these pains go way back in time, before your current or recent relationship, all the way back to childhood. We think it is our partner's job to soothe these pains to finally help us feel whole, but if you think like this, you'll be running the hamster wheel forever. You see, it is our job to reprocess and heal these emotional pains from childhood. There is no ignoring it or running away from it. The answer is from within,"

and then offered his services (Yang, 2022).

Needless to say, the message from the video stuck with me; it hit me like a ton of bricks because it literally explained the adult connections I've had. Brian's message made me realize that maybe my childhood wasn't so perfect after all. Once I decided to share this information with my therapist, whom I lovingly call my PBF (Professional Best Friend), and do my own research, I began to understand more about childhood trauma and CEN. The dismissal of my feelings, lack of affection, disinterest in who I am, persistently being faulted, and emotional unresponsiveness are all examples of some of the CEN I experienced. By no means am I trying to point the finger at my parents for emotional neglect; understanding and accepting trauma is not about assigning blame but processing childhood experiences in healthy ways. Trauma healing is about recognizing how past events currently affect your adult life and learning how to change those behavioral patterns into beneficial alternatives to have the best future. In America, about 60% of adults report having experienced some form of abuse or neglect during their upbringing (Mental Health Connection Statistics, n.d.). Trauma from childhood may initially feel too painful to be uprooted. Still, there are methods that you can use on the journey toward healing. Unveiling childhood hurt is a necessary part of becoming a healthy and responsible person. As long as you avoid dealing with your past wounds, the trauma will find a way to influence every area of your life. You deserve better than living in the shadow of the unpleasant things that happened to you as a child.

Childhood trauma is delicate, and it requires gentleness and compassion to heal. Some wounds are generational, and they've been transferred from one family member to the next, which makes them painful to unpack. Give yourself kindness and grace on your path to healing and be the adult your inner child needs to grow up. This is your opportunity to rebuild and learn how to trust yourself again. Revealing your trauma and understanding it gives you a chance to heal it. Inner child healing will enrich your life and help you restore emotional balance; this is where the journey begins.

THE JOURNEY TOWARD HEALING: UNVEILING CHILDHOOD TRAUMA

How to Overcome Childhood Trauma is a comprehensive journey through the complex landscape of childhood trauma and the path to healing. Using a blend of scientific research, psychological insights, and heart-rending personal stories, the book offers a deep understanding of the diverse forms of childhood trauma, its profound long-term impacts, and the lingering effects it can have on adult life, particularly on mental health and relationships. But this isn't just about understanding your trauma—it's also about transformative healing. Here, you'll be equipped with robust strategies for building resilience, understanding and accepting past experiences, and releasing trauma. Think of each chapter as a way to guide and support you to rediscover your identity and establish a strong self-image by taking steps to set yourself free from childhood pains. This is a resource that gives you permission to love and care for yourself more effectively. Setting boundaries, fostering healthy relationships, and feeling empowered are all things to be revealed on your journey toward healing. Many of the tools provided are dedicated to overcoming setbacks, maintaining progress, and thriving after trauma. This is an essential roadmap for you as someone seeking to work through the pain and navigate healing with gentleness, this is an essential roadmap for you. The inner child is ready to feel safe and cared for again, and the adult self wants to thrive without the burden of a broken heart. With the promise of a fulfilling life filled with joy and personal growth, this book allows us to walk through this together. Two or more are better than one. If you've ever doubted your ability to overcome your past, you've come to the right place; this is the start of something new. Now that you've received a taste of what's to come, let's dive into the mechanisms of childhood trauma.

1

UNPACKING CHILDHOOD TRAUMA

After all, who isn't a survivor from the wreck of childhood?

— NICOLE KRAUSS

Everyone goes through a childhood experience that shapes who they become. Still, the willingness to unpack the emotional baggage sets the survivors apart from the victims. Emotions can get heavy and overwhelming when left unprocessed, which can store negative energy in our minds and bodies. When we don't unpack our trauma, it builds up in the subconscious and unconscious mind, making choices for us throughout adulthood. Unprocessed feelings about wounding childhood experiences stunt our ability to have a healthy emotional flow. Keeping an emotional wound untreated has damaging effects, such as body dysmorphia, depression, etc. Anger, sadness, fear, and shame must be addressed to prevent them from becoming the center of our encounters in adulthood. Our state of mind influences our careers, happiness, well-being, and everything in between. When trauma is dictating our choices, we run the risk of making decisions that cause more harm to ourselves than good. Uncovering hidden trauma allows us to face these feelings while slowly reinstating the balanced flow of emotions; processing is the healthiest response to childhood wounds. But if you aren't aware of the abuse you endured as a child, as in the case of emotional neglect, it may take some time to bring things to light.

CHILDHOOD EMOTIONAL NEGLECT: THE PRICE OF NOT CARING

Experiencing emotional neglect during childhood is a form of maltreatment and abuse that tends to go unreported. Child neglect isn't always obvious because very few people truly know what to look for, including educational, physical, medical, and other types of neglect. This form of childhood trauma can be a devastating experience that damages one's sense of belonging, capacity to trust, and ability to build strong connections. Maltreatment of this nature also results in health conditions that can be difficult to control as an adult. The degree of abandonment children who experience CEN face can range from extreme domestic violence cases to completely dismissing a child's presence. Parenting that doesn't consider the child's needs allows children to engage in harmful behaviors. Refusing to seek treatment for medical or emotional issues a child experiences is also a form of neglect. Being deprived of a healthy connection with parental figures, especially maternal nurture, plays a part in CEN. If someone is born to parents who are emotionally unavailable or unwilling to care for them, it's emotional abandonment, too. Though the form of trauma experienced through neglect may not be overt, it is just as detrimental to a child's well-being as any external form of trauma.

Research indicates that psychologically maltreated children can have the most versatile range of mental health issues within the child neglect category. Emotional abandonment is associated with adverse outcomes for a child's self-image, body, and cognitive development, which are considered acute consequences of this type of trauma. Neglect can also delay a child's ability to build skills for healthy emotional regulation. One of the unfortunate realities of emotional abandonment is that it's often carried through generations. Individuals exposed to neglectful parenting styles are more vulnerable to repeating the same pattern as parents. Outward signs that a child is experiencing neglect are bruises, physical ailments, and other injuries. On the other hand, emotional neglect is more subtle, but people who suffer from it can show unique behavior patterns. A few symptoms of emotional neglect in childhood can include:

- Passive or aggressive behavioral patterns.
- Anger toward parents or guardians.
- Negative interactions with parental figures.
- Delays in language development.
- Poor interpersonal relations.
- Avoidant behavior.
- Persistent feelings of shame, self-loathing, judgment, and humiliation.
- An irrational need for attention.
- Low emotional knowledge.
- Isolative attachment styles, such as insecure-avoidant and disorganized attachment.

Later chapters will explore the multiple attachment styles associated with neglect more deeply. Unfavorable mental health outcomes and long-lasting emotional effects are linked to poor early brain development. The amygdala is the region of the brain that's responsible for retaining information and emotional intelligence, and neglect causes an imbalance in its functioning. Exposure to abandonment causes the amygdala to grow in volume, affecting the brain's arousal and emotional cues, resulting in higher reactivity. Depression, bipolar disorder, anxiety, and phobias are all common psychiatric conditions connected to emotional neglect. People who come from a background of neglect are twice as likely to develop these conditions than those who grew up in secure homes (Li, 2023). In extreme cases, child emotional maltreatment can trigger symptoms of autism, such as self-soothing and patterned rocking (Li, 2023). If any of this sounds familiar or the symptoms strike a nerve, you must consult a clinician for further assessment. A specialist must provide final diagnoses of any mental and physical conditions.

Even in the case of CEN, working to recognize how you were violated in your upbringing will hurt, but it will also get you closer to your sense of self. As you unpack trauma, it's crucial not to personalize the experiences but to move through them instead. Feel the different emotions, register them neutrally, and then let them pass through you. Before you can do that, you need to confront the feelings by fostering gentle understanding. Allowing your emotions to flow rather than suppressing them is always better. Because most adults experience a degree of childhood trauma, having a deeper understanding of it and the types and realities you face in adulthood helps to overcome the trauma. Unpacking childhood hurt is essential in self-discovery and improvement, so let's take a closer look.

CHILDHOOD TRAUMA: A CLOSER LOOK

Trauma is complex, particularly in the case of adverse childhood experiences (ACEs). Early trauma can leave a negative impression on you that shifts your interpretation of the world.

Also, childhood pain is subjective to the person experiencing it. Trauma at a young age can look like living with caregivers who aren't mentally, emotionally, or financially fit to care for you—as in the case of CEN. But trauma can also look like witnessing something terrible being done to someone you love or adapting to complex life changes, such as the separation or divorce of your parents. A closer look gives us insight into some things we can watch out for in understanding and healing childhood trauma. Lingering trauma impacts the way you process life and show up in relationships. You can develop multiple defense mechanisms that you may be unable to explain due to trauma. Here are some coping strategies that are commonly expressed by people who are dealing with trauma.

DEFENSE MECHANISMS FOR TRAUMA

Because traumatic events are so complex, and the brain shapes up to become more reactive, it can cause us to develop defenses to protect ourselves from repeated cycles of emotional pain. Defense mechanisms are mannerisms that we embody in the way we think or act, often led by the subconscious mind. Painful memories are stored in the "reserve," which is what I like to call it, or rather, the subconscious part of the mind. Buried deep down in us is often an understanding of how life works, which directly shapes how we express ourselves and what triggers us. Our defenses can be helpful or damaging depending on the situation and how we use them. Moments of stress can trigger defense mechanisms because the body processes these as distress calls. Whether it's a real or perceived threat, the moment your mind senses panic or hears the distress call, it rushes to put your guard up. Defense mechanisms can be categorized into two primary concepts, broken down into subgroups (Grande, 2021). Primitive and mature responses comprise the main categories, with subgroups that include denial, regression, outbursts, repression, and many more. Perhaps taking a closer look into some of these will help you identify your defenses so you can heal them.

Primitive Defenses

Your initial reaction to being hurt or disappointed can be described as primitive; these are defenses that are impulsive or reactive—almost at the moment—and have limited long-term influence. Children and adults who are still growing their emotional capacity to cope with stress more effectively are usually prone to these types of reactions. Here are some examples of primitive defense mechanisms.

Denial

Refusing to accept the reality that trauma has happened or is still happening is being in a state of denial. This mental state is often associated with the comfort of looking the other way rather than facing painful experiences head-on. When someone is in denial, they refuse to acknowledge the issues and prefer to act like it doesn't exist. Avoidance, projection, and emotional suppression are all primitive responses that develop from an attitude of denial. People can use denial to cope with traumatic memories and distress. An example of this is someone with an addiction problem who refuses to recognize the damage that substances are causing to their life and behavior. Ignoring the problem doesn't serve anyone, not even you; it intensifies the issue and develops more devastating long-term problems.

Emotional outbursts

The process of acting out to express a feeling or thought that's causing internal frustration, anxiety, or fear is described as an outburst. A person may have emotional outbursts because finding an effective way to express their feelings is challenging. Aggression or outbursts reveal the intensity of momentary feelings, which can be addressed appropriately with the correct tools. But if aggressive behaviors and outbursts are left to fester, they are long-term issues. Being angry or upset about something can lead emotionally unstable people to express themselves by punching a wall or throwing stuff. Though momentary outbursts provide quick relief, they are not sustainable in the long run. So, finding ways to deal with childhood trauma is essential in preventing unwanted, long-lasting turmoil.

Projection

Projection is taking your emotions, feelings, and thoughts about something and painting them as someone else's. Projecting is an escape mechanism because putting your emotions on someone else gives a temporary sense of relief. It allows you to create space between yourself and the feeling, which provides you with the chance to express unwanted emotions without taking ownership of them. An example of this is someone in an exclusive relationship accusing the person they are with of cheating without any basis for that accusation. More likely than not, the accuser in this scenario is probably the one who desires to step out of the relationship. The accusation is a chance to express a personal thought without owning it.

Avoidance

Refusing to deal with people, places, or situations that cause discomfort can be described as avoidant behavior. Shame, anxiety, and guilt are feelings that are associated with avoidant behaviors. Someone who has experienced humiliation during a speaking gig might never want to address large audiences when another chance to talk on a public platform presents itself.

Dissociation

The act of denying mindfulness is known as dissociation. Someone with this defense mechanism is prone to psychologically and emotionally detaching from present situations. Dissociation is common with trauma conditions and is usually an unconscious response to multiple real-life situations. Losing track of memories and time, or disconnecting from reality, allows the traumatized part of you to ignore any reality that feels unpleasant. People from violent and abusive childhood environments are more prone to experiencing dissociative behaviors. Trauma, whether it is hidden or uncovered, causes feelings of anxiety that make us want to retreat into ourselves as a way of forcing a sense of safety. Though primitive reactions are short-term expressions, they need to be addressed and dealt with at the moment. When these defenses are left to become constituted patterns, they can develop into more problematic long-term behaviors. Let's explore what that would look like as defenses progress from primitive to advanced or mature defenses.

Mature Defenses

When harmful mechanisms aren't addressed and corrected, they can mature and become long-lasting defenses. Advanced defense mechanisms can make it hard to go through life with ease. The anxiety you feel from trauma tends to be at its highest during the mature stage of your defenses. Suppression, compensation, and deflection are just a few examples of mature coping mechanisms; let's take a closer look.

Suppression

The intentional act of blocking unpleasant feelings, memories, and thoughts from surfacing is known as suppression. Someone who suppresses emotion consciously avoids the feeling or tries not to entertain it. Anxiety and guilt are common emotions that people try to avoid dealing with; therefore, they tend to be the most suppressed. For example, you may be hurt about something that a friend did, and instead of addressing it, you pretend to be okay and continue with your day.

Overcompensation

The practice of doing more than necessary to make up for perceived weaknesses can be referred to as overcompensation. It's constantly going out of your way to do extra to prove your belonging to yourself and others.

Deflection

Using lightheadedness in serious or anxiety-provoking situations to avoid feeling uncomfortable is an example of deflection. Humor is usually used to defect from the pain or hurt within situations like this. For example, telling a funny story during a therapy session as soon as the topic becomes too painful to reflect on.

Sublimation

The process of behaving inappropriately, unacceptably, or in a way that isn't self-aware is known as sublimation. Some examples of sublimation in action include punching a wall, yelling, or aggressively turning your back on a conversation. Redirecting energy towards misbehavior and inappropriateness allows trauma to go undetected.

Learning new ways to cope benefits how we process life and its situations, so addressing the defenses we use will help us do that. Guards aren't good or bad. Instead, they are methods of shielding ourselves the best way we know how. Give yourself grace for how you've learned to manage situations as you uncover and understand your trauma. Your upbringing has sometimes left an imprint that will take time to unlearn, but you are worth every second. Let's address some of the attachment styles that we learn as children, which play a role in the defenses we form.

TRAUMA-BASED ATTACHMENT STYLES

As children, our caregivers are the first example of how relationships should work. How we are treated by the adults we trust during childhood influences the style of attachment that we embody as adults. It also impacts the attachment we gravitate towards when we choose our relationships. Here are some examples of multiple attachment styles that can manifest during adulthood.

Secure Attachment

When we feel safe because our needs are met and understood, a secure attachment style usually comes to the forefront. Securely attached children feel confident of the bond shared between themselves and their caregivers. There's confidence there that when they need something, the primary provider will show up and meet their needs. But trauma steals that security from us. When we grow up in distress or experience unmet needs, we drift further and further away from secure attachment.

Insecure Avoidant

Any insecure form of attachment is a consequence of experiencing disruptive patterns of intimacy. An avoidant child learns that their parent won't be there when they need them. Children become avoidant from believing their caregivers won't meet their needs, so they should ignore their desire to connect. Insensitive and neglectful parenting approaches tend to create insecure-avoidant attachments in children. Child emotional neglect is an effective example of a situation that can cause avoidant attachment. Parental unavailability is scary and damaging to a child.

Insecure Ambivalent

Lack of secure connection creates the belief that one should continuously expect disappointment, which isn't the best way to go through life. An ambivalently attached person is resistant to developing anything more profound than what meets the eye. So, they avoid real and happy emotions connected to valuable relationships. Self-soothing and calmness can also be difficult for ambivalent attachment styles to do. Security and safety almost feel untrustworthy to someone who has learned to attach this way. Parental inconsistency is the marker for ambivalent attachment styles because one minute, the caregiver is present, and the next, they are distant, which creates internal confusion for the child.

Fearful-Avoidant Attachment

Another attachment style that begins in childhood is the disorganized or fearful-avoidant attachment style. It's also a form of insecure attachment marked by extreme difficulty trusting others. Childhood trauma, neglect, and exposure to abusive behaviors are the most common reasons for developing this type of attachment. Fearful-avoidant or disorganized behaviors tend to occur as a mirror for the caregiver's inconsistencies during one's upbringing. Anxiety and avoidant behaviors in adults and children are usually good markers for fearful avoidance. The disorganized attachment style can manifest as contradictory or confusing behaviors and the inability to manage one's emotions appropriately. Fearfully-avoidant people can switch from independence or being removed from relationships to being clinging and desperate for love the next moment. Disorganized attachment usually makes people's behaviors feel unpredictable as they struggle between wanting a connection and being too afraid to form secure relationships. Insecure attachment styles are more closely linked to being neglected or having unmet needs and can result from childhood trauma. Next, we'll explore how trauma can show up in adulthood.

HOW TRAUMA AFFECTS YOUR ADULT LIFE

Past wounds can transfer into the present, as repressed childhood trauma can create complex issues in adulthood. You may wonder how your trauma affects your happiness and adult connections. Perhaps you want to adopt new habits but have no idea where to begin. This section of the chapter lays out some of the defensive and unhelpful behaviors you can look out for in your adult life. All of which are associated with experiences of childhood hurt.

Unfounded Distrust in People

Distrust is prominent in adults who haven't healed from their childhood hurt. During a stage of your life when the world was supposed to make you feel safe, it didn't, so feelings of distrust and questioning are common in adulthood. Early experiences of betrayal, neglect, disappointment, and abuse can lay a foundation for trust issues, which can easily make you believe that the world is at war with you. Trust issues can lead to hyper-independence, isolation, and self-sabotaging behaviors. For example, you may ruin good things for yourself by wanting things to end on your terms. Healthy relationships may cause you to create conflict to prove to yourself that good things aren't forever. Being untrusting can resemble starting an argument with your friend or partner over the smallest things. It can also manifest as eavesdropping on their phone calls and trying to investigate the way they communicate with others through texts and messages. Trauma can increase defensiveness because your nervous system is so used to being on high alert. It can make you believe that you are better off by yourself and that people aren't worth trusting. It can negatively influence your ability to self-regulate and keep healthy relationships.

Poor Quality Relationships

Being highly defensive, avoidant, and untrusting automatically reduces the quality of relationships you can have. At the heart of connection is the ability to exercise trust and free communication as you learn how to build secure bonds with other people. Struggling to maintain this openness and trust with people tends to be a barrier to vulnerability. The inability to be vulnerable with people can make it challenging to exercise empathy and fully commit to relationships, leading to a lower quality of connection than when you allow yourself to be vulnerable. A poor-quality relationship can resemble strong, unhealthy interactions such as yelling to communicate something or persistent dismissal of someone else's emotions. Rolling your eyes while someone is talking or cussing at them can signify emotional dismissal. Trauma weakens your ability to trust, and it intensifies childhood insecurities that may not have been addressed before. That's why dealing with past hurts is valuable in improving the quality of your relationships. However, when you allow yourself to be vulnerable in adulthood, and that connection doesn't work out, trauma can easily convince you that no relationship ever will. You can start to believe that inconsistency and unavailability are things that you should expect from people, though this isn't true.

Misuse of Substances

Feeling isolated or far removed from healthy connections can result in substance abuse. A common sign that you may be misusing substances is hiding or denying your degree of consumption. Say you consume about four to five glasses of wine daily but feel ashamed, so you tell people you only have one or two. Self-denial, lying, and hiding the truth about your consumption patterns can be a massive indicator that you're bordering on substance misuse. People who struggle to engage in positive interactions with people are more vulnerable to turning to substances to numb feelings of pain and loneliness. Traumatic experiences don't automatically mean you'll begin to misuse substances; they just make you more susceptible to them. Remember, when you experience difficulties you struggle to cope with can create a need for escape. Substances tend to be the go-to remedy for people who are emotionally wounded.

Difficulty With Memory and Concentration

When dealing with trauma, it's often difficult to access memories from childhood. Lost memories and the inability to recall are significant signs of emotional repression, a defensive mechanism associated with trauma. Memories tend to be blocked out for chunks of your childhood as a way for your mind to protect you from the pain you experienced during that period. Difficulty recalling childhood memories can be proof of dissociation, which is the process of detaching from your experiences, thoughts, and emotions, sometimes even your body, all in response to trauma. Remembering specific details about an event that changed your life may be challenging for you. Also, having difficulty concentrating is a form of detachment from the present. When your mind wanders, your thoughts and feelings can freely roam and daydream, which may feel better than being attuned to your reality. It's an example of dissociation. The desire to detach and feel nothing is part of why some adults will struggle to the point of abusing substances, which can cause physical illnesses and ailments.

Psychological and Physical Pains

Victims of childhood trauma are 2–5 times more likely to battle mental and physiological issues compared to those who have secure upbringings (Shafir, 2022). Early experiences of pain can create an environment for emotional suffering, manifesting in depressive symptoms and chronic anxiety. It can result in sleepless nights and hypervigilant energy, which tempers with the ability to experience peace.

Equally, untreated trauma can cause physical illnesses like heart disease and autoimmune disorders. Taking care of your emotional needs can so easily aid your physical health. That's why taking this journey toward healing is so important. Knowing how your trauma has impacted and continues to affect you is the first step to building resilience and gaining healing.

STORY: DR. IBRAHIM KURDIEH

Before we can unpack what resilience looks like after trauma, let's explore the real-life story of someone who has experienced and overcome early childhood adversity. Ibrahim Kurdieh's story will be used as a reference throughout the book because he is someone who witnessed abuse and was also beaten by his father throughout his childhood. One encounter he shared of this is when he was eight years old. His parents and siblings were outside, having forgotten their house keys, and Ibrahim was charged with letting them in. But as time went on, while he waited for his family to return home, he started to doze off on the couch and lost all sense of urgency as sleep began to take over. Something so harmless, some would think, wouldn't have resulted in what happened next. Ibrahim woke up to loud, banging noises on the window of his home; it was from his father's furiously balled-up fists, knocking in a rage for Ibrahim to let them in. With shock and sudden panic, Ibrahim made his way to the door with remorse for having fallen asleep and his family waiting outside for a while because of it. Before he could say his apologies or get a word out, his father walked through the door, pushed him to the floor, and started beating him as an outlet for his frustration. Events like this happened frequently in Ibrahim's life. That trauma was permanently colored by the sound of his mom begging his father to stop. Through all that violence, Ibrahim still worked to become a successful psychologist, life coach, and philosopher (Kurdieh, 2019). However, he has been forthcoming about the lasting effects that childhood trauma can have on adult life, relationships, and choices.

BUILDING RESILIENCE

Establishing ways to build resilience is vital in trauma healing because it equips you to feel your emotions without being consumed. Resilience is the process of increasing adaptability in the face of challenges and adverse situations. It's part of empowerment that allows you to bounce back from setbacks and reclaim your stability. Building resilience doesn't mean you stop experiencing difficulties or stress; on the contrary, it means you find healthy ways to cope with unwanted situations. The process highlights your ability to overcome stressful experiences in a way that betters you. Though dealing with adversity may come easier to some people, it can be learned and mastered by those who struggle. So, if you have yet to have the best experience with bouncing back, you can learn how to. Building resilience is essential because knowing how to face challenges allows you to handle whatever life throws at you more gracefully and intentionally. Improving the way you approach difficulties will only increase your confidence and peace. It will profoundly and positively shape your life experiences, too. Here's how to build on what you have to become more resilient over time.

Welcome Change

Not much is certain in life; change is the only thing you can count on. Change is inevitable, and embracing it will attract ease and resilience into your life. Welcoming change involves accepting that everything in life, including yourself and your relationships, must change. Embracing these changes allows you to be flexible and adapt as the differences begin. Flexibility helps you to be more able to cope with difficult situations, which is a cornerstone for resilience. When you welcome change, it allows you to flow through hardships and collect the lessons that come without regret or fearfulness. Next time you're tempted to resist change, permit yourself to lean into it by accepting it as a natural part of your development.

Focus on What You Can Do

Concentrating on what's in your control reduces stress in your life. Childhood trauma can easily cause you to lose perspective of what's in front of you and cause you to focus on things that cause distress. But focusing on what you can do rather than what you can't empowers you to make actionable and healthy decisions. It helps you keep a positive attitude toward the changes and experiences in your life.

Keep Things in Perspective

To minimize overthinking and overcompensating, learn to keep things in perspective. The little things that are happening from day to day can't compare to the bigger picture. Just because you may struggle with something right now doesn't mean it won't get easier over time. Stop putting so much pressure on your life experiences and yourself.

Be Proactive

Waiting for things to happen isn't a bold way to live life. To build resilience from trauma, you need to be a proactive person who plans and puts things into action. The more you do, the more self-trust you'll build. Proactivity also prevents avoidant behaviors that are associated with trauma. If a task seems too big, train yourself to break it down into digestible chunks that you can take on from day to day. Manageable steps are far better than trying to accomplish everything all at once. Your healing matters, and there are many more tools still to learn that will help you build resilience and heal from trauma. The next chapter carries a more positive aura, with tools to help you accept what's happened and move through it.

2

THE HEALING JOURNEY— UNDERSTANDING AND ACCEPTING

Trauma is personal. It does not disappear if it is not validated. When it is ignored or invalidated the silent screams continue internally heard only by the one held captive. When someone enters the pain and hears the screams, healing can begin.

— DANIELLE BERNOCK

Derived from the Greek word "τραύμα," also meaning "wound," trauma is an experience that can destabilize emotions and negatively shape relationships. The Greek description honors how emotional wounds can form within us when we have felt persistent pain during our upbringing. Manifestations of trauma can vary from person to person, depending on how we are brought up and our encounters. Early exposure to situations that stretch our capacity to cope, such as abuse, conflict, or neglect, can result in complex, chronic, or acute forms of trauma. Childhood is a fundamental and impressionable stage of our lives because it represents the period when we are the most vulnerable to being wounded. So, experiences of trauma during this time can leave us with damaging memories and mistrust that follow us into adulthood. A majority of the American adult population has been affected by childhood trauma, so none of us are alone in this (Roncero, 2021). In this chapter, you'll learn how to recognize and understand the childhood trauma in your life, which will help you accept and release your past experiences.

A better version of yourself will emerge through processing childhood trauma. Tragic one-time encounters, such as car accidents, violent attacks, unexpected injuries, and repeated stressors, can result in trauma. Childhood can be a stressful time where all you need is stability, certainty, and emotional care. Still, life isn't always fair to provide these needs. Bullying is a typical example of an experience that can contribute to childhood pain; unfortunately, many have faced this beast as children. Growing up in a household where your parents or guardians constantly fought can also damage your view of the world and yourself. Any encounter or experience that pulls the rug of safety from beneath your feet during childhood can interfere with your sense of belonging and security, which is how trauma develops. Understanding individual traumatic experiences can provide insight into your triggers, which can empower you.

UNDERSTANDING YOUR TRAUMA

Feelings of trauma indicate your emotional response to a threatening, fearful, and powerless event or situation. No hierarchy to one has it worse than anyone else because each person's experience is significant. Traumatic events are complex and delicate and can be ongoing or involve single moments. An example of ongoing trauma is childhood emotional neglect, whereas a car accident describes a single event. These examples also show how trauma doesn't always leave visible scars or injuries. Still, the wounds can be emotional and linger for a long time. Developing effective strategies to recognize and understand your trauma comes with time and intention. Though there isn't a linear method to uncover hidden pain, there are some tools that you can implement on your healing journey. Use the following suggestions to help you discover and heal hidden trauma.

Groundedness and Body Scanning

Grounding is the process of being mindful, which allows you to feel the emotions but not be overcome by them. To begin this process, you need to find a calm and quiet place where you can sit without interruption. Once there, close your eyes and take meaningful deep breaths to prepare for awareness to enter your body. To initiate awareness, you can squeeze and relax your muscles to feel the heaviness in your body. Recognize your sensations as your trauma communicating to you. Permit yourself to feel connected to the floor beneath you as you sink profoundly and closer into the earth. The energy flowing through you needs to be noticed, so hear it. Respecting this moment of grounding allows your body to feel centered so you can truly begin to tap into the subconscious mind where your trauma resides. During this mindfulness practice, give yourself a safe mental space to recall a recent situation that upset you. Focus on what the emotion is communicating, then shift your focus to what provoked you to feel this feeling. As you reflect on the event that upset you, go into detail: What was going through your mind? Can you connect this feeling to an instance in your childhood? As you begin to feel the discomfort of recollection, don't fight it but lean into it.

Be mindful of the ground beneath you and remind yourself that you are safe and on a solid foundation. As you continue to feel the sensation, give yourself a moment to scan through your body for information. Though trauma can leave physical and psychological scars, it can be healed like any wound. When it comes to healing past wounds, knowledge truly is power. No trauma is too powerful to be transformed through healing practices. Learning to recognize and address childhood trauma in your life requires willingness and commitment to go through the hard stuff. There is no avoidance or games, just inner work. The journey is all about knowledge, acceptance, and self-compassion.

Go to Therapy

Loneliness is common during trauma healing, so getting the emotional support you need in the process is crucial. Getting external, professional assistance will be helpful. A mental health clinician can help you heal deep wounds and improve mental fitness, positioning you for healthy relationships with others. Working closely with someone trained to understand the effects of childhood trauma can pinpoint your pain points while helping you transform trauma into positive experiences. Seeking professional help is a way to support your journey toward healing by working with an objective person to create healthier perspectives. You can use cognitive behavioral therapy (CBT), narrative exposure therapy (NET), and psychodynamic therapy as gateways for healing and empowerment. CBT centers around establishing a connection between your behaviors, thoughts, and emotions. It is used as a tool to help you overcome unhelpful patterns of thinking and responding. Alternatively, NET treats ACEs by identifying a chronological pattern of events so you can point out the source of pain and heal from it; this type of exposure therapy focuses on the root cause of traumatization to liberate you from those memories.

Unlike CBT and NET, psychodynamic therapy addresses the hidden or unconscious mind to uncover the meaning of trauma and then use the information to understand where you become stuck in it. Therapy is effective because it can be informed by the multiple approaches explained above.

Therapy sessions will bring better insight into your experiences as they work to guide you in managing your experiences, seeing how they've affected you, and exploring a plan for healing. Creating healthy coping strategies to manage past trauma can build empathy, increase confidence, and push you toward success. Therapy is an opportunity to see life from an objective, solution-based lens. It also allows you to share your experiences with someone qualified to help you. The more you share with your therapist, the more objectively you'll begin to see your experiences—empowering you to rise above them. It will also motivate you to develop self-awareness, which can only be facilitated through introspection.

Practice Self-Reflection or Introspection

The psychological process of looking inward to assess your thoughts, emotions, ideas, and perspectives is known as introspection. Allowing yourself to explore your inner environment is an essential part of healing because it will enable you to identify things about yourself that may be triggering. Self-reflection brings your emotions and memories to the forefront, allowing you to grow from them and adapt to challenging situations. Other advantages of introspecting include more feelings of happiness, promotion of mental health, and increasing your level of empathy. Though these are all great, remaining in a state of self-examination can be detrimental if you obsess over your psychological processes. You can use the tips below to prevent issues like rumination (aka overthinking) and biases.

Explore the "What"

Reflection is about asking yourself questions that explore your emotions and thoughts. Still, in doing so, it's crucial to create a safe emotional space for yourself. Honor your feelings by asking "what" questions rather than "why." Studies indicate that exploring the "what" is a more effective way to promote healing than anything else. For example, when you feel sad, ask yourself, "What is making me feel sad?" instead of, "Why am I feeling sad?" Doing this can create a safe and nonjudgmental inner space for you to process your healing, providing more mindfulness and self-awareness.

Do Nothing

In a world that encourages busyness, taking time off can be healing. Your mind is so full of responsibilities and thoughts that doing nothing offers you downtime. Dealing with trauma can be exhausting, but taking the time to do nothing can remove you from distractions and quieten your mind.

Practice Mindful Thinking

Greater mindfulness can be accomplished through journaling, meditation, and walks. It's a way to keep yourself present and positively aware of everything happening within and around you. When you introspect, it allows you to explore your mind and feelings without drifting into regret for the past or anxiety for the future. Mindful thinking helps you to remain in the now as you analyze each emotion.

Get Curious

To expand your knowledge of your emotions, you need to embrace curiosity. Doing that will increase your understanding of your preferences, emotions, and purpose. Getting in touch with your curious side exposes you to new, unfamiliar territory, which will work to increase your confidence and improve your sense of self. Next, let's take a look at journaling your overwhelming feelings in the spirit of introspection.

Journal Strong Emotions

From the body scanning section, once you've regained consciousness, allow yourself to write the experience down. Journaling is a form of processing that can help heal strong emotions. To understand what you felt during grounding, find a relationship between your emotions and physical sensations. Did you experience any tension while you were recalling a painful memory? How did various parts of your body feel? Assessing this association will empower you to name the emotion. Labeling your feelings will give you a better perspective and understanding of your triggers, which increases self-awareness. Once you've named each emotion and association, permit yourself to approach it with care. To love yourself toward healing involves embracing your pain with the tenderness it needs. You need to express your self-admiration through the pain of the past. When you feel your subconscious take over, consciously bring yourself to say, "This feeling is hard, and I love myself for processing it." Make sure to name the emotion in this statement, and here's an example: "This sadness is hard, and I love myself for processing it." As you can see, understanding your emotions means bringing them out of hiding. After you've done the difficult work of uncovering, you can begin the process of self-acceptance.

ACCEPTING YOUR TRAUMA

Naming your emotions helps you love yourself in the process of overcoming them. Trauma acceptance doesn't mean justifying what happened or even that the feeling of dread entirely disappears. Instead, acceptance is the path toward recovery; it's [1] about releasing the desire to control, judge, and wish things were different than they are. Accepting your trauma is about embracing negative emotions as teachers and guidelines for your needs rather than fighting against the lessons. Practicing acceptance is making the radical decision to let go and step into a state of observation without condemnation. It encompasses embracing the present reality, accepting the past has been painful, and acknowledging that a beautiful life can exist after trauma. Only by doing those three things can you genuinely walk into healing.

The Role of Acceptance in Healing

Recognizing what you are feeling through mindfulness allows you to regard your emotions with the greatest compassion. Your trauma combined with nonacceptance is a recipe for misery, but acknowledging and accepting your pain leads to emotional upliftment. The role of acceptance in healing is to help you see that you are far more than trauma tries to make you believe. Accepting your trauma and stepping toward healing involves releasing thoughts and feelings that go against your acceptance. Leave the "should haves," "would haves," "what ifs," and "musts" out of your vocabulary. For example, saying, "What if it didn't happen?" or "Things couldn't be this way" can impact your ability to grow and accept your experiences. Shifting your mentality from this sort of thinking toward hopeful and optimistic thoughts helps you be more grateful for the things that you have. Acceptance invites more positivity into your life, and you can use the following strategies to help you get started.

Strategies for Acceptance

Normalizing your emotions requires being open and creating a safe space for yourself to experience discomfort without resistance. If you sit with your emotions, they'll eventually pass through you because feelings come and go. In that passing through, you'll cultivate a keen sense of awareness of your needs and what truly matters. Acceptance can also restore the energy you need to actively and consciously work to meet your news. Here are some tips that can help you embrace your past and accept what it is so you can heal.

Cultivate Mindfulness

As a form of meditation, mindfulness is the practice of being intentionally aware of your feelings and momentary sensations from a nonjudgmental perspective. You practice mindfulness by being fully present where you are and noticing what you're doing rather than being overwhelmed or reactive. A range of things are encompassed in mindfulness cultivation, and some examples include breathing techniques, guided imagery, and relaxation exercises. Breathing techniques refer to any calming action that allows you to focus your breath. For instance, diaphragmatic breathing involves inhaling and exhaling to use your lung capacity. During this practice, you can place your hand over the top part of your stomach, where the muscle is, and breathe in until you can't anymore—hold—then exhale until you can't anymore. You can also include counting to make this exercise more effective; so, do 10–15 counts per inhalation and exhalation. Guided imagery, on the other hand, is a practice that's usually used in therapy. It involves focusing on a specific sound, experience, or object to relax your mind. Thinking or imagining yourself in a peaceful place, doing the things you enjoy, is an example of guided imagery. Usually, your therapist or coach will use their voice to guide you to a secure mental place. This guidance would be along the lines of, "Close your eyes, imagine yourself at the beach..." and so on. Guided imagery can improve your quality of sleep and is known to ease anxiousness. Technically, it's also a relaxation technique. The aim of cultivating mindfulness is to help the body and mind relax and reduce stress so you can remain present while accepting your feelings. Mindful living can increase your sense of peace, compassion, and happiness over time.

Foster Self-Compassion

Being kind, thoughtful, and considerate of yourself is known as self-compassion. Mindfulness, body scanning, therapy, and introspection are all tools that you can use to foster self-compassion. Essentially, this is about facing your deepest feelings with kindness and grace. Extending compassion to yourself will help you through your healing journey by protecting you from self-criticism and shame. It's okay to be here; healing and fostering self-compassion remind you of that.

Practice Appreciation

Once you have cultivated self-compassion, it will lead to a better outlook on life. Appreciation is the exercise of being thankful for what you have. Gratitude is important because it turns what you have into more. When you're feeling sad or down in the dumps, practicing appreciation can shift your attitude toward everything you have rather than focusing on what is lacking. Journaling what you enjoy about yourself, your life, and the people in it can help to spark this appreciation. Shifting your mindset this way can help you overcome the intense feelings associated with your upbringing. Awareness of how childhood has impacted your life will move you into a breakthrough.

RELEASING YOUR TRAUMA

Embracing mindfulness, journaling, and all the other tools we've touched on is also a part of releasing trauma. After acceptance comes letting go; that is when a breakthrough happens. Letting go of the trauma that has been overwhelming you for a while is essential to your growth. Since trauma can be stored in the body, releasing it will ease headaches, jumpiness, chronic pain, and dissociation. Even if you aren't always aware, the body can remember trauma long after the mind has processed it. Trauma may manifest as feeling overwhelmed, muscle tension, chest tightness, difficulty sleeping, and brain fog—among other things. Fortunately, healing past wounds is possible through multiple techniques that connect the body and mind.

Techniques for Releasing Trauma

Experiencing ACEs can shrink your window of tolerance, which refers to the limitation that trauma imposes on your capacity to cope with difficulties as time passes. Distress tolerance is essential for effective problem-solving and peace, but early encounters with adversity reduce this level of adaptability. Bottom-up processing can be used to regulate the nervous system, which refers to strategies targeted at the physiological symptoms of trauma. It's a form of processing that allows the prefrontal cortex to regain balance over time, to make it possible for you to re-establish feelings of security. Button-up processing also offers you a chance to engage with your thoughts, logic, and reason as a way to overcome adversity. Trauma-focused therapy, eye movement desensitization and reprocessing, and somatic practices are all techniques that can be used to expand tolerance and release trauma.

Trauma-Focused Therapy

The name gives this one away: Trauma-focused therapy refers to any specific form of processing intentionally targeted at relieving and healing adverse experiences. Multiple types of treatments have a trauma focus, which can include cognitive processing therapy (CPT), prolonged exposure (PE), and trauma-focused cognitive behavior therapy (TF-CBT). PE and CPT are at the frontline of trauma therapy because they have been the most studied and used. They've also demonstrated the highest levels of effectiveness. Prolonged exposure is about helping you confront the source of your fears frequently enough to become desensitized. The disclosure process enables you to work through pain until it no longer affects you with the same intensity. Cognitive processing, however, involves altering your perspective about the traumatic event and why it occurred. The thoughts and beliefs you've developed from ACEs have impacted how you interpret things, so CPT challenges those understandings. Next is also a trauma-informed strategy.

Eye Movement Desensitization and Reprocessing

As a form of trauma-focused therapy, also known as EMDR, eye movement desensitization and reprocessing aim to reduce the emotional charges associated with traumatic memories. This therapy involves the use of rhythmic bilateral stimulation to promote trauma healing. Bilateral stimulation uses rhythmic prompting on the left and right sides of the brain to help your mind form new associations. EMDR connects your body and mind to more positive sensations, which allows you to adopt an adaptive approach to healing. Desensitization and reprocessing involve changing the beliefs related to traumatic events to your benefit. It may be helpful to find EMDR specialists to help you get started on this trauma-processing strategy.

Somatic Therapies

Somatic therapies aim to help you recognize personal symptoms of trauma, safely revisit overwhelming memories, and draw on the available resources to overcome difficulties. Allowing yourself to process through somatic therapies will leave you feeling empowered.

IBRAHIM'S STORY CONTINUES: THE ONGOING IMPACT OF CHILDHOOD TRAUMA

Though Ibrahim and other trauma survivors can find ways to cope with the pain of childhood adversity, building resilience doesn't undo the damage that has been done. CEN and other forms of trauma have lasting effects on us, both physical and cognitive. Survivors of childhood trauma tend to have memories and flashbacks of these experiences. It takes a while to get to a place of acceptance and truly let go.

The Physical Impact of Childhood Trauma

If you've suffered anything like Ibrahim did as a child, then you'll know exactly how that type of abuse begins to distort your beliefs about yourself. Battling a negative self-image and seeing yourself as undesirable is a common byproduct of suffering neglect and traumatic events at an early age. As Ibrahim shares, his life was never quite the same after childhood. The memories of his father turning his young body into a punching bag impacted most of his life and significantly altered his ability to see himself positively. He started to develop a negative perspective of himself that made him think he was fat, ugly, and often unworthy of healthy treatment. He struggled to believe it even when he received feedback from people outside his family who said positive things about him. Poor posture and looking down on himself became his place of safety, "I unconsciously told myself that if I hunch my back and roll my shoulders forwards, then I will seem less of a threat" (Kurdieh, 2019). Not carrying himself confidently started eating away at his body image until he eventually preferred to stay hidden. Though Ibrahim didn't develop eating disorders or autoimmune issues, many survivors of childhood trauma tend to. A disproportionate number of people who have survived ACEs try to find relief for poor self-image by either avoiding food or having too much of it, which leads to all kinds of physical illnesses such as obesity, high blood pressure, diabetes, and a range of eating disorders. These physical battles that occur as a response to trauma also translate into emotional or cognitive effects.

The Cognitive Impacts of Childhood Trauma

Low self-image is one way to erode an individual's mental health. When you experience ongoing mistreatment, neglect, or severe punishment as a child, it negatively impacts how you interpret the world. It makes you start to see people from a trauma-colored lens, so you can quickly go through life as a shell of yourself—similar to how Ibrahim did. He explains that for most of his life, he saw the worst in every situation and expected the worst from everyone who came into his life. Thoughts of the future were filled with pessimistic ideas due to his trauma. Ibrahim's story serves as a tale for many of us. We go through life denying the good because all we've known since childhood is how to embrace the negatives. "My thinking had become very inflexible as the world appeared to me in black and white. I was a victim in a world full of perpetrators, with the occasional savior who came along to rescue me," Ibrahim admits (Kurdieh, 2019). Childhood trauma forces many of us to adopt an attitude of defense, which keeps us from trusting that connections and experiences can be reliable and healthy for us. As in Ibrahim's case, he mentally began to embody the posture of curling up in an attempt to protect himself from the blows of his father's fists. We start to believe that the world is unsafe; therefore, we need to shelter away from it. Yet, this very belief is what hurts us further, turning us into people who struggle to relate and grow resentful toward others.

The Emotional Impacts of Childhood Trauma

We can begin to feel isolated as we pull away from the world and sabotage healthy connections. Feeling alone only increases the rage, fear, and despair that we experienced in childhood and confirms our original biases about the world being a threatening place. Survivors of ACEs have a higher chance of developing mood disorders due to the emotional toil of growing up in hostile environments. Emotionally, trauma can cause hypersensitivity to negative feelings and completely dismiss positive ones. Anxiety, major depression, and obsessive-compulsive disorders are a few manifestations linked to childhood trauma's emotional impact. Though each childhood trauma is different, Ibrahim's story shows the detrimental effect of dealing with adversity early on: "As a child, fear, rage, despair, overwhelm, and confusion were my near-constant companions. As an adult, I struggled with anxiety and depression. Though I seldom experience them anymore, I still have to be on guard to prevent them from happening" (Kurdieh, 2019). When ACEs are left unmanaged for prolonged periods, they can create inner misery, which trickles into external relationships.

The Relational Impacts of Childhood Trauma

ACEs undermine experiences of secure attachment and reliable relations, so they attract us to the negative aspects of connection because they are familiar. So, we become highly anxious, avoidant, and fearful throughout our relationships, making it hard to form genuine connections with people. Fortunately, each person can change their story and move from trauma to healing by confronting the issues that have happened. When you start to understand, accept, and release your trauma, you can begin to build a strong sense of self-esteem and confidence.

3

BUILDING A STRONG SELF-IMAGE —REDISCOVERING YOUR IDENTITY

The past is not simply the past, but a prism through which the subject filters his own changing self-image.

— DORIS KEARNS GOODWIN

Self-image is about the perception you have of yourself based on the things that you've been through and experienced. It's part of the self-concept within psychology, an umbrella concept for all things self-related. Self-image and other terms such as self-esteem, self-confidence, and many more exist. Harnessing the power of positive thinking and self-perception after trauma is essential to understand better and improve your outlook on yourself. What you see when you look in the mirror and what you think about the type of person you are is all related to your self-image. This perception considers how you see yourself from an internal and external position. Having a healthy sense of self means you have a positive interpretation of who you are and your appearance. So, your thoughts, actions, and ideas will reflect that aspect of confidence. Though closely linked under one umbrella, self-image and self-esteem can be distinguished because one goes more profoundly. Self-esteem encompasses the level of respect you feel for yourself; it involves how good or unfavorable you think about your self-image. Having low self-esteem is likely to correlate with poor self-perception. Though self-esteem and image are closely linked, these are independent concepts of the self.

Your self-image is connected to your confidence; low self-confidence can affect every area of your life. Low self-esteem can affect your relationships, work ethic, and well-being. To begin building a strong self-image, you first need to recognize the situations that impact your confidence. Think about your triggers, ranging from work and school to romantic and platonic relationships. Childhood trauma plays a part in the level of self-esteem that you can build within yourself. In this chapter, we explore the importance and role of self-image and how it's connected to our mental health and relationships. It will also unpack how self-image is affected by childhood trauma, how it can lead to recurring trauma, and ways to rebuild self-image.

UNDERSTANDING SELF-IMAGE

As self-image is your perception, it includes your body ideas, gender, and self-expression. Not only does self-image refer to how you think about yourself, but it also encompasses the way you'd like to be. Particularly as it pertains to your personality, ideal self, skills, values, and principles; your self-perception is determined by what you think you offer to society. It's also influenced by societal norms of masculinity and femininity that you may or may not identify with. The self-concept provides a broader, abstract perspective of how you view yourself. Your self-image is a more concrete and measurable idea of who you are. You learn to define and see yourself based on your behaviors, thoughts, and interactions with the world. This exposure allows you to shape yourself beyond abstract and ideal concepts continuously. Many mental health endeavors and topics are centered around the idea of bettering self-image.

An example is body dysmorphic disorder, which occurs when someone pays careful attention to perceived weaknesses and imperfections—actual or nonexistent—in their personal traits or physical appearance. It happens often at the cost of their self-image and confidence. How one perceives oneself is an essential part of one's existence. It can influence the success of external relationships and impact their sense of belonging and well-being. Having a poor self-perception can lead to multiple sabotaging behaviors, many of which include self-harm, self-deprecation, and destructive thinking. But understanding what self-image truly entails can help prevent all of this for you.

Three components comprise self-perception: How you think about yourself, what you think other people think about you, and how you would like to be or be perceived. The latter is best known as the desired or ideal self. Within these components, broader suggested dimensions are labeled as the physical, psychological, intellectual, skill set, moral, and sexual dimensions. Each one allows for great insight into the term self-image, as explored in the book *Society and The Adolescent Self-Image* by Morris Rosenberg. The physical dimension focuses on how you assess and interpret your appearance, which is linked to how you look, feel, and think you should look or feel.

On the other hand, the psychological dimension is determined by your personal qualities. In other words, your personality and cognitive processes are encompassed within this aspect. The intellectual dimension is determined by evaluating your understanding and intelligence; where you place your competencies and capabilities is usually connected to this part. For example, if you think you are smart enough or not, it's all determined by your intellectual aspect or self-image.

However, the skill set dimension determines how you interpret your social and technical skills. It is all about how you see yourself and what you can bring to the table.

The moral dimension differs from the skill aspect in that it turns inward. This dimension of self-perception evaluates your values, beliefs, and principles—all the things that are a compass for your life. Lastly, sexual dimensions determine how you feel regarding normative identities. Some questions to help you understand are "Do I fit the societal expectation of who I am or should be?" or "Am I more feminine or masculine?" The by-product of the thoughts, influences, and behaviors that you developed throughout your life work to inform your self-perception. Experiences, as early as childhood, begin to shape how you see yourself and, thus, proceed to present in the world. That's why childhood trauma can be so detrimental. A child who was exposed to violence or bullying at school is more likely to develop a low self-image based on what they were mocked and teased about growing up. If the other kids laughed and joked about how big of a head you have, you're likely to carry that sense of shame into adulthood. Tough childhood experiences can shape the development of unpleasant self-image narratives. All is not lost, though, because self-perception can be changed and improved through effective techniques. Adopting nonjudgmental patterns of thinking, meditating, and cultivating a positive attitude toward your life and the people in it can help uplift you and transform your poor self-image. Let's take a moment to look at the interplay between self-image and childhood experiences.

CHILDHOOD TRAUMA AND SELF-IMAGE

Children tend to internalize every experience that happens frequently in childhood, so if abuse is all you've been exposed to, it can become a part of your identity as an adult. Experiences of CEN or any ACEs can skew the way you view yourself. Your confidence, self-awareness, and self-worth are at the core of your self-image. What trauma does is chip away at those fundamentals, negatively impacting your self-perception. Self-reflection begins in childhood; we learn how to express ourselves and the multiple ways we can emote. We also learn what we enjoy and aren't necessarily good at; all of these things serve the purpose of building or damaging our self-image. For someone constantly exposed to childhood trauma, your self-image becomes more lopsided toward the negative experiences.

When that shift happens, it makes seeing yourself in a positive light hard. Due to past traumas, you can consciously and subconsciously see yourself as endangered and the world as threatening. How you're brought up and exposed to detrimental experiences can cause a ripple effect that makes you see the world inaccurately. You can quickly develop negative and mostly untrue perceptions that make you fearfully live your life. A child who is offered a secure attachment when growing up has more of an advantage in life. In that, being taken care of from an early age makes it possible to develop healthy patterns of thinking that allow for an accurate self-image to form. But when you're constantly faced with adversity from a young age, it has the opposite effect. Self-image is hugely linked to a child's first point of validation, care, and acceptance—which is supposed to be the parent or primary caretaker. Yet, when you don't receive that safety, as in the case of childhood trauma, it creates a negative belief and self-assessment. These early encounters can stunt or damage your ability to see yourself in a hopeful, reliable, and empowering way. Below are some ways that you can start to rebuild a damaged self-perception.

REBUILDING SELF-IMAGE

People who feel a sense of belonging and embrace and experience a sense of self-acceptance tend to extend self-compassion. When you have a positive, more caring outlook, it will boost your self-perception immensely. Self-image is rebuilt through resilience. You must routinely convert setbacks into bouncebacks by continuously pushing yourself to see the good in every circumstance; practice making lemonade from lemons. When you face your obstacles with the attitude of growth rather than despair, you set yourself up for a positive self-outcome. If turning setbacks into achievements sounds overwhelming, you can start with one area of your life that's important to you. Then, once you've proven your capabilities in that area, continue the pattern into other parts. The point is that it's always better to take things one bit at a time until you reach your goal instead of trying to take on overwhelming chunks. Studies on self-image have shown that it is possible for all types of people, no matter how low they start, to improve their self-perception (Nickerson, 2023). There are multiple ways to rebuild your self–image, and these are the tips you should keep in mind.

Take Up Nonjudgmental Reflection

Start to see things from a neutral perspective. Taking up nonjudgmental reflection will help you overcome tough emotions from trauma. Loving-kindness meditation can help you reframe your poor self-image and unhelpful thoughts into more positive and healing processes. This type of mediation uses a constructive and reflective approach to accepting reality. Nonjudgmental reflection means cultivating greater mindfulness of damaging thought processes and habits and using this to facilitate unconditional, positive regard. A way to do this is by shifting your negative perceptions to more positive dialogues, which will be assessed more deeply in the following sections. You can develop a more significant and positive capacity for how you see yourself by simply applying the following tips to your life. Loving-kindness is about taking care of yourself, mentally and physically, to increase your sense of worth and connectedness.

Form Healthy Habits

Exercising, eating well, and maintaining your well-being contribute significantly to your self-image. Physical activity will improve your health and ensure you look and feel good about yourself. Exercising releases positive hormones into your body that make you more prone to having a positive outlook. Also, creating a routine that allows you to clean and moisturize your skin and brush your teeth twice a day is part of forming healthy habits. When you actively take care of yourself, it communicates to your mind that you're someone you hold in high regard. The more you care for yourself, the more your self-perception will become. So, incorporate some nutrition into your life, go to the dentist, book a psychology appointment, and even join a jogging club to help you get the positive emotions flowing. Let's explore how you can include confronting your inner voice as a part of building your self-image.

Call Out Your Inner Critic

Stop speaking so unkindly to the wonderful person that you are. Sure, there are things you can improve and others that aren't perfect, but you are a valuable part of this life despite it all. Childhood trauma makes it easy to create an identity around hopelessness and worthlessness; it can cause you to question every aspect of who you are. It can also make you doubt your achievements and abilities, but calling out your inner critic is a way to confront these negative narratives about yourself. Just because you grew up being told you are "lazy and good for nothing" doesn't mean you need to identify as those things today. Confronting the inner voice that constantly tries to remind you of how insufficient you are is a significant step toward healing. You need to face all of the negative stories you've told yourself and trace them to a source. Perhaps the self-belief that you aren't smart enough was a seed planted around peers during childhood. Then, it was watered as you continued to develop. Maybe each time a teacher corrected your homework and your parent shouted at you for getting the answers wrong; it solidified this negative understanding of who you are. By calling out your inner critic, you proclaim that you will no longer answer that negative belief anymore. Instead, whenever the thought "I'm not smart enough for this" creeps in, you permit yourself to say, "I'm learning right now, so it's perfectly okay not to know how to do this yet." Vocalizing to yourself that your contributions and skills are forever growing will help you become less hard on yourself. You can personalize this scenario and apply it to areas of your life where you need to practice calling out to the inner critic. Once you've gotten into the habit of challenging the internal narrative, you can start to become more attentive to your strengths and values.

Pay Attention to Your Strengths

What are you good at? Too often, we need to focus on the right things or the things that we need to improve on. Yet, imagine the power you'd harness within yourself if you took the time to focus on the advantages of being you. In the same way, everyone has things they could work on and improve, which is how we all have positive attributes. If you're battling to identify your own at this moment, it may be a sign that you've been beating yourself up for far too long. Paying attention to your strengths means acknowledging the good things you contribute to your work, personal relationships, and the people around you. Take the positive affirmations others have told you, and try your hardest to start believing them for yourself. When you can point out your strengths, it frees you from trauma attachment. You begin to see yourself as more than what has happened to you; there's healing in that. Rebuilding your self-image will require patience, love, and self-care, which are fundamentals that will be explored in the following chapter.

4

SELF-LOVE AND SELF-CARE— NURTURING YOUR BODY, MIND, AND SOUL

The thing that is really hard, and really amazing, is giving up on being perfect and beginning the work of becoming yourself.

— ANNA QUINDLEN

Trauma can overwhelm your ability to feel secure and safe in situations. Unresolved stress and emotional pain can create a sense of disconnection and self-criticism that can only be relieved through cultivating a sense of security for yourself. Practicing self-love is the best way to calm the analytical mind that reminds you of your traumatic experiences. Nurturing your mind, body, and soul is a reflection of loving and caring for yourself. Everyone can be compassionate, which is the key to fostering a trauma-informed approach to healing. Trauma-informed care is essential in helping you make sense of your history. Many professionals use this approach to support you in addressing difficulties from childhood. True healing can't happen without love and care at the center of your experiences. That's why using this approach in your personal life is crucial.

To continue understanding your trauma with an unconditional and nonjudgmental attitude, you need to be willing to practice self-love and care. These two concepts are important ways to pour into yourself and your self-concept. The empathetic understanding of your imperfections and weaknesses is self-love and care. You need to embrace these components to have an emotionally healthy and positive change in your life. Multiple facets of success are influenced by your ability to love yourself through the challenges in life. The pathway toward a more satisfying and happy life is taking advantage of self-care and love strategies. The compassion and love you show yourself will increase your self-image and heal your memories of ACEs. This chapter will explore the importance of self-love and how it can facilitate the healing journey. Learning how to practice self-love and self-care is essential to healing childhood trauma.

THE POWER OF SELF-LOVE

Self-love is a catalyst for positive change and personal growth. Understanding the value of loving yourself will propel you toward healing. The multi-billion-dollar industry is dedicated to self-care and love. Still, bath bombs, gift baskets, and massages aren't the only way to express love. It is not how you build self-love. Childhood trauma, complex relationships, and multiple situations that make you feel hurt may make it challenging to love yourself. The good news is that loving yourself is a skill that you can build and improve. The power of self-love is immense; this form of care can help you override pre-learned behaviors and habits that have been solidified by trauma. Loving yourself is about learning to appreciate everything you've been through and creating a positive regard for yourself.

Self-love and self-esteem are closely related because caring about your well-being increases your confidence and outlook toward yourself. Unlike self-indulgence and narcissistic behaviors, self-love isn't about being self-absorbed and having a diluted self-interest. Instead, loving yourself is powerful because it increases your awareness and empathy. While narcissist traits are associated with poor mental health, loving yourself contributes positively to your life and those around you. Having high self-esteem correlates with loving yourself, and it all positively affects your overall well-being, mental toughness, and connections.

The power of self-love is also in that it releases you from some of your negative, untrue beliefs about yourself. Traumatic experiences can make it feel like you aren't deserving of good things, but self-love reminds you otherwise. It helps you hold yourself to a high standard without adopting perfectionism. Self-love allows you to live life with self-compassion, which makes it possible to have the drive to accomplish goals and the grace to overcome your shortcomings. Loving yourself brings an unconditional component to living your life, allowing you to forgive yourself for your mistakes and the things that have happened to you in childhood. Self-love is powerful because it's the acknowledgment that you deserve the best despite all that you've been through. You aren't ever too hurt or wounded to practice loving yourself. Isn't that the biggest relief? Multiple studies suggest that self-love is crucial to taking action, chances, and new opportunities. Truly loving yourself opens up your entire world to everything you couldn't have imagined otherwise; that's why putting it into practice is essential.

PRACTICING SELF-LOVE

Loving yourself is rooted in science; there are various advantages to treating yourself well. Some of these benefits include building higher resilience and reducing stress levels. When you love yourself, it helps you feel less stressed because it makes you feel more confident in what you can accomplish and move through. So, when facing challenges, you are more likely to approach them calmly and confidently. Negative feelings and being self-critical work to build up anxiety and trauma in your life. Yet, self-love makes it possible to see solutions and positive outcomes, which makes it easier to quickly get through problems. Loving yourself hinges on whether or not you like yourself enough to work on improving and doing the things that bring joy into your life. When you approach life with self-love, you can also love others better. In theory, practicing self-love may seem less overwhelming than when you're expected to put it into action. Here's how you can start cultivating a self-love journey.

Implement Positive Self-Talk

Having a positive internal dialogue goes hand in hand with the practice of self-love and compassion. The words you speak about yourself reflect the type of self-talk you have become accustomed to. You learn what to think and believe about yourself from a very young age; this ties in with self-image development. Your subconscious mind influences your inner voice, which is significant in revealing what narratives, thoughts, and ideas you've grown to believe. This way, your internal dialogue can be both helpful and damaging to your mental health. Having good things to say and recognizing your weaknesses as things to work on can characterize a positive outlook on yourself. When you adopt encouraging self-talk, it can create an internal environment of hopefulness and optimism. Many reckon that self-talk depends on personality, suggesting that more naturally optimistic people are likelier to adopt an excellent inner dialogue than people more prone to pessimism. Even so, everyone can work to create a more helpful inner dialogue, regardless of personality. Some may need to work harder to facilitate a growth mindset than others. Positive self-talk can increase your quality of life and give you a more progressive outlook on challenges. It can make you a healthier person emotionally, physically, and in many other ways.

To start a positive dialogue, you need to identify the barriers you have to think in a helpful manner. Notice the internal dialogue that keeps you from achieving positivity in your life. Negative self-talk can come in many forms, the most common being personalization, magnification, catastrophizing, and polarization. We all fall victim to believing that everything that happens in life has to do with us. Personalization is an unhelpful pattern of processing that makes you think that you are at fault for everything.

An example of this is a friendship, where you gave your all in, comes to an abrupt end. Personalizing this outcome looks like picking out the things that you could have done better to convince yourself that your actions are the reason the relationship ended. Another example is taking someone's post personally because it addresses something you've shared. We personalize many reasons because we believe that all trauma and events of our upbringing were warranted. Magnifying, on the other hand, is the negative pattern of paying attention to the negative aspects of every situation while completely disregarding the good. Say you receive feedback from your boss, for example, and eight out of nine comments are positive, but your mind focuses on the one that isn't. Typically, this thinking pattern is tied to not believing that you can be enough for anything or anyone, which couldn't be further from the truth.

On the contrary, catastrophizing is the pattern of thinking that focuses on the worst possible outcome despite the facts or reasons that may present otherwise. Here, you can believe that you aren't skilled at anything, even when your co-workers constantly point out your amazing contributions to the team. On the other hand, polarization makes you see the world as one thing or another—there's no in-between. It is the belief that everything is inherently good or bad, with no room for a middle ground. Once you recognize which processing pattern you fall into, it'll make it better for you to adopt a more positive attitude. Self-compassion is essential to changing your thought processes. Here's how you can adopt positivity through your actions and inner voice.

Reframe Your Inner Dialogue

Changing your words from negative speech to positive takes time and effort. You need to have more than just intention to ensure your processing becomes more positive than negative. Implementing positive self-talk will take practice; the following examples will support you as you reframe your inner dialogue.

First Example

• Negative self-talk: "If I change my mind about this, I'll disappoint everyone."

• Reframed positive self-talk: "Changing my mind is something I have the power to do. Besides, others will understand."

Second Example

• Negative self-talk: "I failed and humiliated myself."

• Reframed positive self-talk: "I tried, and I'm proud of the progress I've made and the courage I displayed with that decision."

Third Example

- Negative self-talk: "I can't wear that because I'm overweight or out of shape."

- Reframed positive self-talk: "I am capable, strong, and in control. I will wait to wear this for a healthier version of myself."

Realizing some of your personal thought processes, which may not be serving you, will help you overcome childhood trauma, be self-compassionate, and flourish in your life.

Be Kinder Toward Yourself

Treating yourself with kindness will help you build more resilience than when you belittle and shame yourself. Compassion empowers you to be bold about your life and to leave all of the hurt from the past where it's supposed to be. It's about having enough courage to overcome the urge to sit in your pain for too long and permit yourself to live a life outside your trauma. Being kinder to yourself, especially when it's not easy to, is revolutionary. Self-compassion can look like creating humor in the most unpleasant situations because laughter can heal your heart. Don't get me wrong, you don't want to use humor to replace processing your trauma, but rather, use it to get back to yourself every time you get a break from processing. Part of maintaining a positive attitude is doing things that will shift your negative mood to a more positive one. Watch funny videos or comedy shows, be around naturally funny people, and allow your heart to find some sort of goodness in the mess you're navigating through. You don't have to feel heavy or guilty for creating pockets of kindness and happiness for yourself during this time. Also, kindness means adopting more positive self-talk and affirming yourself. Speaking positively about yourself will motivate your thinking pattern to work in favor of the healing you want to see. Another way to care for yourself is by establishing healthy standards or boundaries for your life.

Set Healthy Boundaries

Having standards will allow you to attract the energy that you want to see in your life. Learning to say "no" to things you don't want to do is a way of being true to yourself. Being honest with yourself is at the core of practicing self-love. People pleasing is a form of self-sabotage that can result from childhood trauma. The idea that the only way to keep harmony between yourself and others is to satisfy their every need goes against the principle of loving yourself. Setting healthy boundaries is a way to protect yourself from such vulnerability, and it's a key element of self-love. The main function of boundary setting is knowing what you can give and how much energy you're willing to spend on things. Learning how to care for yourself and give to others without self-abandonment can help you only do things that serve your well-being. Promoting self-care can be done by setting more helpful boundaries, which will be explored deeply in the next chapter.

EMBRACING SELF-CARE

Do you thank yourself as often as you do others? Think about it; it's so natural to say please and thank you to other people, but it can be so much more challenging when it comes to doing it for ourselves. It is because it hasn't been normalized as much as giving care to other people has been. Learning to embrace self-care is about showing gratitude to your body and mind for surviving trauma and helping you live after it.

Forms of Self-Care in Healing Childhood Trauma

Establishing a regular self-care routine will help you take the trauma-informed approach to healing. There are multiple facets of self-care that need attention for you to heal. Taking care of your physical, emotional, psychological, and spiritual aspects will propel you toward the healing you deeply desire.

Physical Care

Move your body because blood flow is essential to creating a healthy mood and helping you heal well. Even so, exercising is one component of physical care. Others include brushing your teeth, eating healthy food, and taking baths. Introducing multiple forms of physical care into your routine will leave you feeling fresh and confident. Start with the basics; mindful movement is anything from lifting weights at the gym to taking a walk or running outside. Whatever your form of exercise is, make sure it gives back to your body by making you feel good. Also, create healthy food plans that will last you from week to week without feeling the urge to get takeout. By taking care of your gut, you ensure that your skin and whatever else makes up the physical remains taken care of. You need to do things that make your body feel good and enjoy yourself while you're at it. Taking your physical care seriously will improve your emotional sense of self.

Emotional Care

Keeping emotionally healthy means doing the things that bring you joy. We spend so much of our lives doing what *must* be done that we forget the magic of doing what we want to do. Your emotional boost will come from prioritizing fun in your life almost as much as you do your responsibilities. Plan dates with your family and friends where you can all just laugh and forget about the troubles of the world. Something about being surrounded by positive energy and doing the things you enjoy will have you healing from trauma much quicker than you can imagine.

Mental Care

Your intellectual and emotional well-being work together to create a healthier version of yourself. If you are looking to include mental care in your routine, you should get comfortable with mentally stimulating activities. Such as reading books, playing mind games, and many more. Mental care is a version of exploring self-love that helps you stay sharp while improving your skills and competencies in life. Go to a bookstore, download a crossword puzzle, or anything else you can think of.

Spiritual Care

Meditation is an effective way to care for yourself spiritually, emotionally, and physically. It is an opportunity to center yourself and overcome stressful situations when life gets too much. Too often, our minds run rampant, thinking about various responsibilities and concerns, but meditation allows us to pause. It helps us turn all our mental and emotional energy into fuel for healing and living quality lives. All you need to do is find a quiet and safe space to close your eyes, breathe, and simply be present. You can include guided meditation in your routine. These can be downloaded as apps on your phone.

An example of this is *Insight Time*, which is one of the best ones out there. This app has five to 60 minutes of meditation to facilitate relaxation and balance. Much like other spiritual practices, meditation makes it possible for you to address your pain without judgment or fear. Other forms of spiritual care include attending church or mosque if you are religious. Prayer and dedicating your life to your faith can be a powerful instrument of healing from traumatic events. Also, listening to music can tap into the spirit and improve your sense of self from within. When it comes to care, it's important to do whatever your emotions, spirit, and body may need; there's no linear way to go about it.

WELCOMING CHANGE BY EMBRACING SELF-LOVE AND CARE

According to Ibrahim's journey, the way out of the cycle of trauma is by embracing a life of healing, but this is a long and hard process. Even so, it is a path worth taking toward self-discovery and genuine self-care. To heal from ACEs, you need to tackle the physical, mental, and cognitive symptoms of trauma head-on. Ibrahim talks about the importance of taking a multidimensional approach to healing, focusing on the body, heart, and mind. Trauma affects every inch of you, so it's only fitting to direct your healing across all aspects. The information above can help you start your journey of welcoming change and embracing self-love and care, and the following content will add to what you already know (Kurdieh, 2019).

Heal Your Body

Yoga, mindfulness, meditation, and exercise are all vehicles you can use to heal the body from trauma. Ibrahim used a range of these to assist in his path toward healing, and you can do the same. Various classes exist that offer trauma-informed movement to help you reconnect with yourself in gentle and progressive ways. Find those places in your area; Google where you can sign up and attend such practices as you work toward healing. Getting involved in practices that heal your body will help you use your breath as a way to restore the balance that trauma took from you.

Heal Your Heart

In his journey, Ibrahim acknowledged that emotional trauma requires emotional healing, one of the most challenging things to do. Healing the heart involves confronting the past to overcome it. There's only one way through childhood trauma: witnessing the scars and wounds of your inner child and then making the conscious decision to clean, dress, and bandage them daily. Understanding your attachment styles, defense mechanisms, and hidden pain is the beginning of your transformation. Somatic therapies, EMDR, positive self-talk, and reframing your cognition are all ways to heal the heart, which have been mentioned in earlier sections of the book. Get proactive in your healing, and you'll see all the positive ways that you'll start to change.

Heal Your Mind

Healing your body and heart plays a huge role in healing the mind. By building resilience, cultivating a positive self-image, and embracing flexible thinking, you make way for yourself to heal the mental aspect. Ibrahim also had to confront mental forms of healing in his journey: "Before healing my mind, I lived in a rigid black-or-white world of false certainties. Now I understand that reality is a space of playful ambiguity to be cherished instead of feared" (Kurdieh, 2019). Allowing yourself to understand your trauma and heal it through CBT, self-compassion, and other forms of self-love will leave you feeling much more accessible today than you did yesterday. This healing journey is something that you should embrace and tackle, one day at a time. In this chapter, we briefly touched on the value of setting boundaries as a form of caring for yourself; as stated earlier, the next chapter will explore this in detail.

5

SETTING BOUNDARIES—TAKING CONTROL OF YOUR PERSONAL SPACE

The more you value yourself, the healthier your boundaries are.

— LORRAINE NILON

Trauma can restrict the safety and control you feel over your life, and establishing rules for how people can and can't access you is a way to lift that restriction. Setting boundaries is about protecting yourself from emotional and physical mistreatment. You can set boundaries by saying, "I don't want x. Instead, I need y." Creating standards for your life ensures that you facilitate positive treatment from the people around you. It allows you to be picky about what you accept and don't so you can cultivate happiness after trauma. Learning to set better personal boundaries is how you preserve healthiness in your life, relationships, self-respect, and other aspects. Boundaries aren't about shutting people out but inviting them to love you appropriately. When you understand and care for yourself, you have no shame in sharing your needs with others. Setting boundaries helps you avoid feelings like shame, resentment, anger, and disappointment caused by unmet needs. As a child, you are less capable of knowing what you need, making it difficult to share your boundaries with others. That's why childhood trauma is so delicate and hard to unpack. As an adult, you become more empowered to learn and address your needs. In this chapter, you'll understand why boundaries are important and how to set your own, and you'll see how doing so can be a form of informed care. Also, once you've set your standards, you will need to maintain them, and how to do this will be addressed, too.

THE NEED FOR BOUNDARIES

Having specific rules and standards for yourself is a form of self-care. Boundaries can take multiple forms, ranging from inflexible or rigid rules to loose and almost nonexistent. With boundaries, it's always better to fall in the middle of rigidness and looseness; these are known as somewhat flexible or healthy standards. Setting healthy boundaries is about knowing your expectations must be clear in several ways. Firstly, your standards must establish what behaviors are acceptable and not from other people. So, what treatment would you approve of from your friends, co-workers, and family? Secondly, your boundaries need to determine what behavior other people can expect from you: What will you contribute to your relationships? Having healthy expectations of yourself and others helps you avoid engaging in toxic relationships that can be emotionally traumatic. When you have healthy boundaries, you may develop a deeper awareness of your basic needs and wants and, therefore, know how to communicate with them better. Setting boundaries also helps you share personal information with others with discretion. Chances of oversharing or giving too much of yourself prematurely become lower when you have boundaries in place. Also, when you establish better rules of engagement, it helps you value your opinions and ideas more. Boundaries can equip you with the confidence to take on whatever life throws your way. It also allows you to accept other people's standards as well.

When you have boundaries of your own, you become less inclined to want to push other people's standards. You learn to respect it when others communicate what they want and need from moment to moment. So, hearing "no" from someone you love feels less like a rejection but rather an opportunity to honor their right to consent. In the same breath, having healthy boundaries makes it possible for you to not under-share with others. You become a more active participant in your life and meet interactions with integrity and clear-headedness.

Your standards are essential, and keeping them balanced is always better, so rigid boundary setting should be avoided. It might look like establishing expectations that keep you withdrawn or isolated from others. It can also manifest as detachment in relationships, whether these are romantic or platonic. Boundaries that are too strict and nonbreathable can cause you to have strained connections with others and result in very few close relationships. Rigid expectations do no good for your trauma because they keep you in a state of loneliness that can damage your emotional health. Setting loose boundaries can be just as damaging as well. When your boundaries are almost nonexistent, it can make you vulnerable to being mistreated and manipulated by multiple people. It can result in resentment and anger toward others because you would constantly be in a position of self-abandoning. Loose expectations can look like getting overly involved in other people's drama or issues to the point where you become consumed by their lives and narratives. Setting loose expectations for yourself and others can manifest as the inability to be clear about not wanting something. You may feel like saying "no" will hurt people, so you avoid it by saying "yes" to things—even when you genuinely aren't interested. Loosely set boundaries lack clarity and intentionality. These can also result in oversharing your personal information with others. Having no concise boundaries can cause you to participate in people-pleasing behaviors without regard for your needs and emotions. The need for boundaries is undeniable, and here's how you can start to foster your own.

ESTABLISHING BOUNDARIES

Boundaries promote a sense of autonomy or control over your choices. Creating boundaries that keep you safe while allowing you to live your life to the fullest is essential. When your boundaries are tampered with or unclear, it can increase the production of stress hormones in your body—adrenaline and cortisol—which can have an adverse reaction. Yet, when your standards are set and confidently shared with others, it gives you peace of mind knowing that you will respect them even when others don't. Healthy standards are subject to change and alteration depending on the situation. For example, you can mix your strict and looser standards to help you strike a balance in your life. So, you may want to set more rigid boundaries at work and more flexible ones at home. Either way, knowing how to set your boundaries requires understanding multiple types of boundaries.

Five Boundary Types: Understanding Your Personal Limits

Establishing boundaries is significantly determined by your understanding of the multiple types. By knowing what boundary forms exist, you position yourself to be more intentional and clear when you work through fostering your own. Everything in your life that's important for your happiness should have its boundary. Let's explore some of the five areas you'd need to set clear intentions for in your life.

Physical Boundary

Your personal space and sense of privacy represent a physical boundary. It is about drawing your line of comfort regarding things like physical touch, displays of affection, and access to your space. Hugs, kisses, and handholding are all elements of your body that require clear boundaries. You might enjoy hugging your friends and family, but not so much your colleagues. So, you can establish that boundary at work by being clear that you prefer handshakes or simply waving at the office. It's important to be upfront about your physical preferences so that people know where the line is. To establish a space boundary, you may set the expectation that when your door is closed, people must knock and wait to hear a response before taking the appropriate action. Knocking for you may help to make you feel safe instead of someone barging into your space unannounced. Physical boundaries have to do with anything that makes you feel taken care of in the spaces that you exist in; it's also a way of protecting your body.

Sexual Boundary

Physical boundaries tend to cross over into sexual aspects. A sexual boundary refers to your expectations regarding intimacy, including sexual comments, gestures, and opinions. Being told that you're "sexy" by your spouse or partner can be exciting. Still, that same comment from your boss is something you'd be discussing with HR. Sexual boundaries allow you to be treated appropriately in multiple contexts. You can also communicate which of your partner's gestures you accept and don't. The sexual boundary is where consent mostly comes into play. The aim of setting these boundaries is to free you from the belief that you need to do things sexually that make you feel uncomfortable.

Intellectual Boundary

Now, let's move from the body to more of the mind. Intellectual boundaries have to do with your thoughts, ideas, and beliefs. You have the right to share views, feelings, and opinions with others and have those be respected. People don't have to agree with what you have to share. Still, they can honor your intellectual boundary by accepting your subjective experiences for what they are. Instances where someone tries to convince you that your experience is "wrong" or your opinion is "unimportant" are examples of this boundary being toyed with. Your emotions and ideas shouldn't be dismissed, talked over, or ignored because they differ from anyone else's.

Emotional Boundary

Your personal feelings make up your emotional boundary. Here, you can communicate with others about how much you're willing to share and how quickly. You might find that you feel comfortable sharing difficult emotions more gradually than you do exciting ones. So, your friend may want to know what made you feel sad on a particular day, but you are in your rights to respond, "I'm not ready to talk about that experience yet." Emotional boundaries ensure your feelings are protected and not forced out of you. Even when it comes to sharing about your childhood trauma, it's okay only to go as far as it is comfortable for you from day to day. That's why you'll never find professional therapists pushing you to share beyond what you can in a session. Emotional boundaries respect that feelings can be hard, so they must be handled with the utmost care. Space, body, and emotions aren't the only boundaries you need to look out for; your finances—which are more material—also need protection.

Financial Boundary

You don't have to spend on things when you don't want to. Your money and what you're willing to spend it suggests your financial boundary. If you enjoy saving your money rather than spending it on frivolous things, you may not want to loan it to someone who doesn't share the same sentiment. Other boundaries can include the time you are willing to share with others and how much access people can have to you. When you are ready to establish your own boundaries, be sure to take each of the listed boundaries into consideration. You may not have always felt protected in childhood, but that power lies in your hands as an adult. Once you've set your expectations, get ready to communicate them in a manner that makes you feel heard and empowered.

How to Communicate Boundaries Effectively

Effectively communicating your boundaries limits your exposure to stress, which protects your mental and physical health. When communicating where you stand, you need to practice assertiveness. It is a term that involves expressing your emotions, needs, wants, and feelings with vulnerability, honesty, and respect. Being assertive isn't about making demands or bossing people around. Instead, it's about speaking in a way that makes it easier for people to listen to your position. You'll need to follow the subsequent suggestions to practice being clear and assertive when setting boundaries.

- Speak with intention, but don't raise your voice. Being loud about your needs isn't the same as being clear about them. You need to learn how to communicate calmly and surely. Using your "speaking" voice rather than screaming or yelling instructions at someone will convey how serious you are about your communication. Yelling makes people want to get defensive, so you must avoid raising your voice when communicating your standards to others.

- Communicate your needs by sharing your desired outcome rather than what you don't want to see. Effective communication is progressive communication, meaning it's future-focused. You'll have better odds at getting what you want out of a situation by saying, "This is my expectation," rather than stating, "This is what I'm afraid will happen." Use positive enforcement when communicating your needs to people, and this can only be done by stating the request.
- Embrace the uncomfortable feeling that arises from staying true to yourself. Communicating boundaries, though healthy for you, won't always feel as good as it should. Sometimes, the body and mind are more inclined to want to please others in the name of "keeping the peace" than wanting to stay true to yourself. But giving into guilt and shame will only make it more challenging to set and maintain boundaries in the future. Just embrace the discomfort early on so you don't have to spend time wrestling with loose boundaries and manipulation in the future.

Sometimes, people push your boundaries simply because they don't like them. You may come across people who find it hard to respect where you've drawn the line, so they may push your buttons to see how much they can get away with. In that case, you'll need to learn how to manage those button pushers by establishing healthy ways to address crossed boundaries.

Dealing With Pushback

When something is done or happens to you, your discomfort often signifies boundaries being crossed. Some people will question why your boundary is there because it's not where they'd put it, and you need to guard against such people. You can rely on your internal alarm system to determine when your physical, emotional, and financial boundaries are violated. Dealing with pushback is vital to building healthy connections with people. There are multiple signs that your boundaries may be getting violated. Some examples include codependency, repetitive boundary setting, and feeling pressured. Codependent behaviors are characterized by one person's needs being met while others are pushed to the side. In codependent relationships, one person tends to fall accustomed to taking on responsibility for both parties. At the same time, the other is left free from accountability. Some common signs of codependent behaviors are conflict, inconsideration, and pleasing the other person at your expense. These behaviors may make it hard for boundaries to be respected and upheld between people, creating resentment and aggression.

On the other hand, a repetitive boundary setting directly reflects your boundaries being ignored or dismissed. When you've expressed your boundaries, but the person's behaviors continue to cross them, it may indicate conscious or subconscious dismissal. People can either forget or intentionally not meet your rules of engagement, and you need to find a way to express your seriousness when it comes to this. Suppose you have to continue to say the same thing to someone over and over again; in that case, it may be time to communicate the consequences of any violations. Feeling pressured into acting a certain way is also a sign that your boundaries are being pushed. Here's how to deal with pushback to get your relationships on track with your expectations.

Clarify The Consequences

To set clear consequences for boundary violations, you must state the outcome of your boundaries not being respected. Should someone continue to cross the line, you need to consider your plan of action to show that you aren't playing. Without consequences, upholding your expectations will be more challenging than it's meant to be.

Be Patient and Consistent

Establishing boundaries takes time, and so does respecting them. Stay calm as you find a way to navigate being heard and affirmed during this period. If you set your expectations, allow an appropriate time to meet them. Also, stay consistent. Sharing your boundaries with others and then relinquishing them communicates uncertainty about what you need. People will cross you when they feel like your standards can be persuaded to change. Consistency means having the resolve to enforce your expectations no matter what, and it applies to every expectation you set in all aspects of your life.

Give Chances: Remind People of Your Boundaries

Again, practice patience and give chances. Even people who want to meet your needs may battle with the adjustment at first. The effort may be there but might need better execution. So, if people forget your boundaries or act in ways that violate them, feel free to give them one or two grace periods where you reiterate your expectations and point out where they are falling short. You can stand your ground during pushback by saying, "Hey friend, I remember telling you that I like XYZ, but it seems you keep forgetting. Please, next time, will you keep to this? Thank you." It clearly states that your boundary has been violated and you aren't accepting the behavior. By the same token, your friend is less likely to feel shamed or belittled into fulfilling your request the next time the same thing comes up.

Address the Violation Calmly

As the example above, letting someone know where they could improve guides them toward satisfying your expectations better. Passively addressing things when you're upset won't change them. You need to be bold and sure in expressing boundaries being crossed. For example, "I know you're upset, my friend, but calling me names isn't the way to go about this. You've crossed a line, and I prefer we talk once the tension has subsided." It expresses your violations calmly so you can maintain good rapport and relationships after the fact. Sometimes, people can continue violating your expectations no matter how often you address them, and you need to discern when it's appropriate to cut them loose.

Remove Persistent Violators

You can't change a person's behaviors; you can only communicate how those behaviors hurt you. People who are determined to continue pushing back, even after being given multiple chances to do better, aren't worth your emotional effort. Suppose someone dismisses how you feel and violates your boundaries persistently. In that case, the best thing to do may be to end the relationship. Removing persistent violators can help prevent any further dismissals of your needs. In doing this, you can still tell the person that you're removing them because they have been unable to meet your expectations, even after numerous opportunities. You can also state that this decision is for the benefit of your mental health. Giving people a heads up before removing them from your life helps you leave the situation without regret or guilt, knowing you gave it everything you had. If you can, shut down your connection with them completely. Persistent violators should no longer have access to your time and energy. Removing these relationships can look like blocking people on social media, deleting phone numbers, and unfollowing what doesn't serve you. Now that you know how to go about establishing your boundaries.

STRATEGIES FOR MAINTAINING BOUNDARIES

Creating positive boundaries is essential for living a satisfying life after trauma. You must first explore your feelings and emotions to start setting and maintaining boundaries. You can use self-reflection to help you address your needs and wants. Being more self-aware can prevent setting blurred boundaries linked to unhealthy lifestyles and lower levels of joy (Pattemore, 2021). Here's how you can maintain your boundaries.

Remain Clear and Firm in Your Decisions

If you don't take your standards seriously, no one else will. Remaining transparent and firm in your decisions is about staying consistent with your expectations. Avoid letting things slide when your needs are unmet because this can lead to confusion and cause people to continue crossing the line with you. Once you've communicated your expectations, be sure to reinforce them throughout instead of bending and breaking your needs to make others comfortable. To help you remain transparent in your decisions rather than backtrack, you should prioritize time for yourself every weekend. When you carve out the time to reflect, you become better equipped to stick to your choices—even when people challenge you. Remaining firm in your decisions also means letting your "no" be just that; don't be swayed to a "yes" or "maybe" when people push and prod.

Handle Guilt-Tripping

Naturally, people want things to happen on their terms, so it's no surprise that you'll encounter a few people who want to see if they can get you to change your mind—don't. Handling guilt trips is crucial to deciding what you want and need. You can still show up and love people without letting them persuade you with their emotions to undermine what you need to satisfy their selfishness. Handle the guilt-tripping by reiterating the original expectation every time someone tries to sway you otherwise. Using language like, "As I mentioned before…" or "I meant what I said…" and then proceeding to reaffirm your position will prevent you from falling victim to the guilt of having standards. Remember also to allow your boundaries to grow just as you are.

Re-Evaluate Boundaries and Adjust When Necessary

Re-evaluating boundaries is based on the understanding that as you develop, so do your expectations. You can't run on the same rules for every phase of your life. Normalize permitting yourself to check whether your boundaries satisfy your needs from season to season. Adjusting your boundaries ensures that you don't miss a beat or have moments when you feel like your needs aren't being met despite the effort that others are putting forward. Your boundaries will help you feel more secure and connected, supporting you in establishing healthy relationships with others. Let's use the next chapter to explore how trauma impacts relationships and what you can do to re-establish positive and healing connections.

Your Chance to Pay it Forward

"It takes each of us to make a difference for all of us."

— JACKIE MUTCHESON

So, you've journeyed through the pages of "How to Overcome Childhood Trauma." First off, high five! And secondly, do you know the superpower you've just unlocked? It's the power to impact and inspire.

Think about this for a second: Have you ever felt that warmth when a stranger helped you, or someone dropped a golden nugget of advice just when you needed it? Yep, that one! Now, how would you feel about being that person for someone else?

Reviews are the magic carpets of the digital age. They transport potential readers to a world they're curious about. Your words could be the light that guides them home.

But why reviews? Reviews are the next best thing! They give folks a sneak peek, a feel, a vibe of what they're about to dive into. Your experiences, epiphanies, and challenges paint a real, raw, relatable picture.

Here's the golden ask: If this book touched, transformed, or even just tickled a thought in you, would you drop a few lines about it? Not for us, not for fame, but for that one person who needs your words to make their decision.

So, are you ready to change a life today? Remember, it takes a village to heal, grow, and thrive. Be a part of someone's village and scan the QR code to leave a review.

6

REDEFINING RELATIONSHIPS—BUILDING HEALTHY INTERPERSONAL CONNECTIONS

People and relationships never stop being a work in progress.

— NORA ROBERTS

Relationships mirror our inner selves; they reveal our needs, wants, attachments, and fears, as well as our strength and capacity to improve. Building healthy interpersonal connections can expose the best or worst in us, allowing us to view ourselves in ways we wouldn't have before. Traumatic relations can damage us, while good relationships can restore and heal us. Many professionals, from philosophers to spiritual coaches and psychologists, understand relationships as a basic human need for our existence. Positive social connections such as family gatherings, hanging out with friends, and joining special religious, community, and workplace activities, are essential for our well-being. Not only do these relationships offer us joy, fellowship, and pleasure, but they also influence our longevity. Multiple studies have shown that having adequate and healthy social circles makes us happier. Positive relations make us more likely to live longer, be fulfilled, and have fewer health challenges. A deeper look into the ideas surrounding the importance of connection suggests that people were never meant to live this life on their own. You and I are supposed to form a community with each other so we can grow and thrive in life. Healthy interpersonal relationships can transform us if we are willing to embrace the process of understanding our trauma, learning about people, and growing through our experiences.

THE IMPACT OF TRAUMA ON RELATIONSHIPS

While positive relationships add to our lives, negative connections detract from them. Traumatic experiences are an example of how relationships can have a harmful and life-altering impact on our lives. After trauma, expressing empathy and affection in relationships can feel challenging. Traumatic situations restrict our range of vulnerability, making it difficult to trust and connect with others freely. Overwhelming emotions are normal in post-traumatic circumstances and can influence our interactions with friends, family, and other social relations. While responses to trauma are unique to each person and linked to their subjective experiences, most people share some common reactions to these difficulties. Patterns of aggression, withdrawal, insecure attachment, and many others are among these commonalities. Traumatic events deeply challenge our sense of safety, which impedes self-confidence, our interpretations of the world, and how we think and feel about people. Social connection can reflect these impediments in multiple ways. Living through trauma can increase hypervigilance, flashbacks, and expectations of danger, betrayal, or potential harm within new and old relationships. These emotions can perpetuate the fear of vulnerability and intensify confusion about what is safe, who to trust, etc. All of this can make it challenging to open up to others; even those who were once trustworthy can be easily mistrusted after trauma. Feelings of helplessness and the loss of control from hard experiences can deter the ability to build healthy connections. Learning how to release your trauma by using the content from earlier chapters, particularly the second one, can help you overcome these feelings so you can begin to form healthy connections.

FORMING HEALTHY RELATIONSHIPS

Healthy relationships require time, energy, and effort to form and maintain, but they also give the same back. Being in good connections strengthens you and leaves you feeling empowered. Toxic relationships, on the other hand, are those that tend to take away while giving nothing back to you. When a relationship isn't healthy, you feel it by how it drains you from your energy. Forming toxic relationships takes all your effort and time and leaves you unable to focus on healthy ones. When you're faced with toxic situations, be sure to cut those connections off. Healthy relationships are about recognizing this toxicity, developing your communication skills, and finding a balance between giving and taking; let's see how.

Recognize the Red Flags and Toxic Behaviors

Some groups of people aren't worth spending time around because they can be more damaging than helpful in your journey toward healing. Recognizing the red flags and toxic behaviors that others may have will help you avoid toxic circles and relationships.

Overcontrolling Behaviors

In healthy relationships, there has to be a good compromise where everyone involved wins. Overcontrolling behaviors like someone wanting all your passwords, wanting to know where you are and who you are with at every second of your day, or blatantly harassing you are red flags. Behavior like this is a common sign that a relationship could potentially threaten your emotional and physical safety. People who use power dynamics to assert themselves and attempt to control your movements, decisions, or ideas are less interested in building with you and more interested in manipulation. Controlling people don't want what is best for you. If a family member, partner, or friend shows you signs of control, whether by dictating what you wear or where you go, this is a red flag.

Feeling Broken Down

If the people around you make you feel broken down, it's a red flag. Healthy relationships should make you feel supported and empowered in your gifts and differences. The people who love you want to see you win, so they will tend to encourage and champion you through life. Something needs to change in your connections if you frequently battle feelings of rejection, lack of support, etc.

Gaslighting

The term gaslighting describes a common form of manipulation, and it's a clear red flag in relationships. It typically serves as emotionally abusive behavior, which makes a person feel victimized by the manipulator who gets them to question their subjective experiences and reality. Gaslighting makes an individual doubt themselves, their sanity, and their judgments. This manipulative action can cause you to feel guilty and ashamed about everything, even when you did nothing wrong. Next time you are around your social connections, be attentive to how you feel and how happy you tend to be—it will reveal a lot.

No Trusted Connections

Your quality of friends and connections is more important than your quantity. What matters more than having a huge circle of people around you is having a good few who see the value in the person you are. It's a red flag when someone has absolutely no connections to vouch for their character or intentions. People who don't have social relationships, even a few of them, can be showing warning signs. Keep an eye out for that. Another way you can form healthy relationships is by communicating with yourself better.

Develop Your Communication Skills

Very little progress can happen in relationships when you don't feel free to express yourself. Forming healthy connections requires good communication, which can be cultivated by offering someone your undivided attention. Developing your communication skills is about improving your ability to pick up on the verbal and nonverbal cues that the speaker is sharing with you. Communication goes two or more ways; each person who is a part of the conversation needs to be given a chance to express their perspective and share their opinions without judgment. Verbal communication refers to the content of words and sounds from the speaker's mouth. Usually, people will use this form of communication to express their feelings, emotions, and thoughts. Communicating with people is a daily occurrence, and it can't be avoided. So, improving how you listen to what people are saying will help you form strong bonds. Listen to the sounds and words from a neutral perspective to prevent hearing them from personal bias. You can do this by making mental notes of the message being shared by the speaker, asking open-ended questions, and paraphrasing what you've heard so the speaker can clarify if you've heard them correctly. Some open-ended questions that you can ask to start a conversation or gain in-depth understanding during one include:

- What's on your mind?
- What's been happening since we last spoke?
- What else?
- Such as?
- What would you like?
- How can I help?

Asking questions similar to the style in the above example will give the speaker freedom to add their thoughts and emotions without feeling spoken for or rushed. If you need clarification on something, ask for clarity or more details; don't make assumptions. The important thing about communicating effectively is taking the time to truly be interested in what's being said. Listen with the intention to find the meaning in the message, and genuinely be curious to spot what new information you could learn from the person who's sharing with you. Also, when you get the chance to speak, do so without interrupting or getting distracted. Do your best to validate the speaker along the way by using positive affirmations; things like, "I hear you," "Uh-huh," or "Yes, that makes sense" can go a long way in showing your interest in what's being communicated. Giving people your undivided attention during a conversation shows how much you care and genuinely want the relationship to work.

Nonverbal communication, on the other hand, makes up most of how we express ourselves. Words matter, but actions and expressions are just as crucial to communication. So, pay attention to how someone's body language communicates with you.

Things like posture, eye contact, facial expressions, and much more are great tools to watch out for. You can often tell if someone is happy, honest, sad, or shy through the way they use their body during communication. Also, be intentional with your nonverbal cues, and avoid things like yawning or fidgeting because they can so easily communicate irritation or disinterest. Now that you have some tips for developing your communication skills, let's go a step further into learning balance in your relationships.

Learn Balance in Your Connections

Relationships are transactions, which means you should give and take just as much as the other person. No single person should be overextended while the other benefits from their vulnerability; this is known as being codependent. Instead, every connection you have should be characterized by two or more independent people who want to contribute equally to the connection. Learning how to strike a healthy balance in your relationships is crucial to their success and maintenance.

NURTURING AND MAINTAINING HEALTHY RELATIONSHIPS

It's easy to read about healthy relationships and their importance, but this is an opportunity to pause and consider *how* you can rebuild relationships and connect with people after trauma. It is a chance to implement strategies to help you nurture and maintain healthy connections over time. You can start the nurturing process by establishing mutual trust, respect, and support. Trust is the foundation for any healthy relationship; without it, toxic behaviors can be let loose to run rampant. When you have a mutual sense of trust, you are more prone to share deeply in the healthy "give and take" pattern of your connection with people. Your trustworthiness and theirs make it possible for you to love deeply, respect one another, practice empathy, and so many more necessary things. In nurturing and maintaining your relationships, exercising trust can look like taking your partner's word for what it is rather than giving in to the urge to snoop around their personal space. When there's trust, there's also freedom. Trusting each other means none of you will try to be their private investigator—snooping to see whether someone is being honest. Instead, you both sit back with ease, believing that the other person has your best interests at heart and wouldn't deceive to save their skin. Trust is also great for conflict prevention and resolution because it lays the ground for mutual understanding. This type of psychological and emotional freedom makes interactions with trusted people more fun. Once you've established trust, mutual respect and support will follow. Here are some strategies you can use in your daily encounters to foster healthy and growing relationships with the people you care about.

Share Experiences Together

Spending quality time with your loved ones is the key to strengthening your connections. One-on-one time with your people needs to be a priority. Life is too unpredictable to hold back on love and compassion; don't allow the hurry and distractions of life to keep you from sharing positive experiences with others. Prioritizing time with people who add joy to your life can help you overcome negative feelings associated with trauma. Laughing, playing, and talking with trusted people can reframe your perspective to see life from a more hopeful and rewarding perspective. Spending quality time with loved ones doesn't need to be anything extravagant; you can give someone a phone call or invite them over for some lunch with you. Shared experiences have a way of reducing feelings of loneliness and increasing feelings of happiness. Investing in others and allowing them to invest in you creates a more joyful internal environment.

Focus on Shared Ideas

As you can tell, Sharing truly is caring. When nurturing and maintaining healthy relationships, finding out what makes you similar is important. Though appreciating what makes you unique is a great value to bring into relationships, focusing too much on differences can make you feel far removed from the people you're connecting with. That's why it's crucial to find out what you may have in common rather than fixate on what makes you different. Focusing on positive commonalities and ideas has profound relational benefits; it makes positive habits and thought patterns flow more easily between people. It does not mean ignoring everything that makes each person unique within the relationship. Instead, make sure to balance those differences with commonalities. Making a habit of finding what connects you makes building a relationship more enjoyable for all parties involved.

Address Issues Immediately

It is important to address issues as soon as they arise in order to prevent bitterness, resentment, and grudges. Disagreements and conflicts in relationships can form a healthy part of growing to understand one another, but this can only happen when all parties don't avoid confrontation. Ignoring issues can make these disagreements and conflicts brew, which can increase the tension experienced between people. You don't want to pretend to be okay with certain things if you aren't because these problems will become more significant issues down the road. To address issues immediately, you need to consider the other person's perspective as an essential part of forming a healthy relationship; this way, you'll handle them with respect rather than out of anger. Empathy, which is considering the other person's viewpoint, will allow you to understand them more and help you build a deep connection. It will also make it easier to address what you aren't happy with and have it received in a positive manner.

Appreciate and Support Each Other

Showing support for each other's goals and contributions will help form closer bonds. You can express your appreciation for people in relationships by finding out what they enjoy and discovering ways to share those things with them. Also, cheer your loved ones on and share your goals with them. Let the important people in your life know their importance and thank them for all they do. Having meaningful and strong relationships is imperative for your mental and physical well-being and a staple for healing. Healthy relationships can cultivate individual purpose, reduce stress, and empower you toward trauma-informed care. When the people around you are good for your well-being, it keeps your mind and energy well-maintained. If you are willing to put in the work to build strong support systems, you'll soon realize how powerful fostering good connections is for your growth. Good people can inspire and cheer you on through the toughest times and experiences; all you need to do is invest in them—and them—in you.

Remember Ibrahim's story: The traumatized mind can lose confidence and make you see things as "all-or-nothing" or "black-and-white," but healthy relationships exist in the balance. Relationship dynamics need triage after trauma; this involves noticing unhealthy attachment patterns and replacing them with functional ones. Ibrahim points out that trauma can result in the development of codependency, where a victim, persecutor, and rescuer are created; he refers to this as the drama triangle (Kurdieh, 2019). All insecure attachments are built on these codependent roles that develop between people during trauma events. Fostering mutually appreciative and supportive relationships frees your mind from the trauma-induced belief that relationships are unsafe spaces and liberates you from perpetuating a codependent pattern of behavior. The persecutor in you is silenced, victimhood becomes empowerment, and the urge to fix or rescue everyone is replaced by the need to save yourself (Kurdieh, 2019). Healthy connections can help you overcome insecure attachments and replace trauma with healing and abundance. Overcoming setbacks, challenges, and obstacles is possible when you feel a sense of belonging. It's also achievable when you've established a healthy inner space; let's take a deeper dive into the topic of obstacles in the healing journey.

7

OVERCOMING OBSTACLES—RESILIENCE IN THE FACE OF SETBACKS

Resilience is accepting your new reality, even if it's less good than the one you had before. You can fight it; you can do nothing but scream about what you've lost, or you can accept that and try to put together something that's good.

— ELIZABETH EDWARDS

It can feel like nothing good comes from our experiences when faced with adversity, especially in the case of ACEs. But hard times build up our tolerance through resilience, which eventually helps us better handle misfortune. Resilience is the process of adapting to life's tough times and challenges. Through this process, we can experience the reward of successfully overcoming difficulties, which can have greater mental, emotional, and behavioral outcomes. The key to overcoming setbacks and trials is flexibility because it's the only way to progress and adjust to external and internal pressures. Of course, obstacles feel a bit more manageable in adulthood than they do during childhood. The main reason is that we've developed more emotional intelligence through adult life experiences. Resilience may not come quickly to most people, but research shows it can be built, practiced, and strengthened over time.

Your journey to overcoming obstacles begins with the optimistic view that no challenge, even your trauma, is too difficult to fight through. Within you, there's an infinite capacity to cope with difficulties and recover from setbacks—you just need to believe that for yourself. Through resilience, you can practice staying calm in the face of adversity as you recognize everything as temporary and a simple part of your story. Overcoming obstacles is about sharpening your coping skills to use what's at your disposal to manage challenges. Examples include asking for help when needed, seeking advice when the bigger picture is unclear, and embracing your mistakes. The uplifting reality of setbacks during the healing journey is explored in this chapter. Here, we unpack how obstacles affect us and the importance of building resilience during seasons of hardship. Strategies for overcoming setbacks are undertaken with special emphasis on using every skill presented so far, such as building resilience, self-love, self-care, and setting while re-adjusting personal boundaries.

THE REALITY OF SETBACKS

It's tough to see the bright side when things seem to be going wrong at every turn. When one obstacle stacks up on top of another, it can feel like you can't catch a break. Each new issue can present as another brick in the wall of stress, trauma, and disappointment, which can be exhausting to keep climbing. During moments of hardship, when setbacks come one after the other, it's crucial to remember that you aren't alone. Most people go through hard times and troubling situations but find their way out. Even the most successful people you know continuously face giants of failure, setbacks, and mistakes. Resilience is making a pathway that feels like there's no way out. If Oprah can overcome an adverse childhood and create a wonderful adult life for herself, so can you! Aside from your willingness to push through difficulties, there's not much difference between you and some of the most successful people you know. You can genuinely build the life you want by overcoming the hard things that life throws at you. Having the resolve to say, "I deserve good things, and I will push past every wall to get there," is how you overcome and succeed in life.

The reality of setbacks is they require you to exercise patience with the expectation that there will be growth on the other side of your adversity. If you are in a tough season of your life and it feels like things are going from bad to worse, tell yourself you will find a way through. Overcoming obstacles is more about your mindset and attitude toward tough times than your ability to get through. Anyone and everyone can bounce back from setbacks with a favorable outlook, including you!

STRATEGIES FOR OVERCOMING OBSTACLES

Building resilience is at the forefront of overcoming obstacles and healing from trauma; this is explored very well in the book's first chapter. When obstacles come your way, it's tempting to curl up and throw in the towel. Your thoughts will have you believe that giving up on yourself is better than pushing through the challenge, but overcoming obstacles is a natural and doable part of the human experience. Self-doubt becomes void when you remember that the most extraordinary people have had to go through their fires, and when they do, they've come out on the other end—unscathed. You are also a great person, and your fire may be scorching hot, but you will also make it to the other side. The first step to overcoming your obstacles is to see them as they are, not as you want them to be. Then, recognize that, in every adverse situation, there's a chance to grow from it. Don't let the expectation of what you want things to be blind you from the opportunity to see your situation as it is. You can use every circumstance for good, even the most disheartening ones. When you accept reality for what it is, you become empowered to cope with your hardships. Here are some strategies that you can use to overcome personal obstacles.

Reframe Your Perspective

Instead of viewing hard situations as unmanageable or overwhelming, reframe your perspective by breaking down the issue into smaller, more manageable tasks. Shifting your attitude from a negative perception of a problem to seeing a positive way through is how you'll overcome setbacks. Feel encouraged to invite hope into how you tackle challenges and learn to see adversity as a way to improve your stress management skills. Calling out your inner critic and practicing mindful reflection, as mentioned in Chapter 3, can be valuable in your attempt to reframe your perspective toward obstacles.

Concentrate on What You Can Control

Resilience is about having a realistic outlook toward challenges but not exercising blame or obsessing over things that can't be changed. When you fixate on multiple things at once, your reality will start to warp. You need to permit yourself to concentrate on what you can control rather than try to take on everything all at once. Focusing on what you can control prevents emotional spiraling and being consumed by negative thinking patterns. Some ways to focus on what's in your control are by creating a checklist to help you break down big tasks into more manageable ones, scheduling all of your responsibilities so you can tackle one thing at a time and writing a list of your priorities. Being intentional about your focus will go a long way in your healing journey.

Build Healthy Habits to Cope with Stress

Creating a routine that helps maintain good physical and mental health is an example of how to build healthy habits to cope with stress. Monitoring your sleeping patterns, eating well, and exercising are essential stress management practices. Physical exercise is an effective stress reliever that can take a moment to do. For example, taking 15 to 25-minute walks a day can increase blood circulation and improve respiratory function. A simple walk allows you to be in the sun to get some vitamin D and oxygen flowing through your body. Trust me, your heart, mind, and limbs will thank you for giving them the break they need. Walks can provide a change of scenery which you can enjoy. Stepping outside your usual surroundings will shift your mind into a different frame, too.

A healthy diet and quality sleep are also good to include in your schedule. Refined carbs, such as cookies, fries, or processed chips, can spike blood sugar. When this spike starts to plummet, the crash may cause you to experience higher stress and anxiety levels. But eating healthier will help to fight this stress over a long period. Protein and naturally balanced foods such as eggs, avocado, and walnuts support your mind and body, leading to better emotional regulation and higher energy. Exercise and having a healthy diet go hand-in-hand with sleep. Studies find that waking up and going to sleep at around the same time every morning and night is beneficial for your sleep cycle. These habits can improve your well-being and help you in your trauma-healing process.

Embrace Support

Letting people in is another way to enhance your well-being. Learn to share your feelings about your hardships with people you trust; vulnerability is another way to build resilience. Having people who support you in your corner is essential to your growth. Embracing support can also give you an objective perspective on your problems and allow you to adopt new ideas to help you manage. Coping with obstacles and building resilience aren't things you have to do without support. If you need help, don't hesitate to talk to your friends and family or even involve a mental health professional. It's okay to need support; even some resilient people need help sometimes. Embracing support from others is a part of overcoming setbacks because it involves knowing when to ask for assistance. Using these strategies to overcome setbacks will also help you prevent and prepare to tackle future challenges.

PREVENTING AND PREPARING FOR FUTURE SETBACKS

By building your resilience and reframing your mind, you've already started preparing for future setbacks. Nurturing the inner child and moving past difficulties take time; unfortunately, there's no smooth elevator ride to the penthouse of healing. In preventing and preparing for future setbacks, you must resign yourself to the fact that adversity can be your greatest teacher. When you face setbacks, you learn to push past self-limiting beliefs by confidently discovering what more you can do to improve. Think back to the chapter on redefining your self-image after trauma, which ties into this: Pushing past your limitations helps you to develop a healthy perception of yourself. By overcoming your obstacles, your resourcefulness increases, and you learn how to hone your skills and develop your strengths by taking on new adventures. The more you embrace challenges, the greater your learning and growth capacity becomes. Other aspects of preventing and preparing for future setbacks include being aware of your triggers, developing a crisis plan, and building your support system; let's take a look.

Be Aware of Personal Triggers

Emotional suppression isn't healthy, especially within the healing journey. Your emotions need to be allowed to breathe freely, and the best way you can make that happen is by recognizing your triggers. Think of emotions as signals that supply endless information about your internal and external environment. Personal triggers are an alarm system of feelings that help clarify what you're comfortable with and what is not. Occasionally, you will find that some emotions can feel stronger than others. Usually, when your feelings cause an internal imbalance or misalignment, that discomfort is referred to as a trigger. Understanding what yours are can help you create a way to cope with them. Personal triggers can be situations, places, people, and things that evoke intense and sudden emotions. Everyone experiences triggers uniquely, depending on how each memory is processed. The brain and body record traumatic experiences and encode them into memories, and when these are stimulated, triggers are formed. In the case of post-traumatic stress disorder (PTSD), triggers are prominent. A military veteran who ducks at the sound of loud noises is an example of how triggers manifest. Even someone who avoids the holiday season because it reminds them of a loss in the family is a lived example of how triggers can come into play. Personal triggers are sudden and can be evoked by multiple sensory stimuli. Symptoms of this can include feeling panicked, hyperventilation, automatic thinking, panic attacks, and physical tension. You can notice your triggers in the following ways.

Recognize Your Emotions

Be attentive to how you feel because triggers can result in overwhelming emotions that can be used for clarity. Notice when you feel down, upset, fearful, and many other feelings, then try to accept and understand the source. It's okay if you can't always pinpoint the source; triggers aren't always straightforward. Just remember to be attentive and patient with yourself.

Listen to Yourself

Attentiveness and patience in recognizing your emotions are part of listening to yourself. If you find yourself constantly thinking about something you believe you have overcome, it could be a sign that it is triggering you. Also, if you tend to have explosive and outsized reactions to things, it could be something you should try to understand. Thoughts, physical sensations, and feelings work together to inform you of how you're feeling, so pay careful attention to them.

Check Your Emotional Temperature

Simply put, check on yourself. Try to spend some time on your own sorting through your thoughts and feelings. You can keep a journal of your daily emotions to monitor how you feel over time. Checking how you are and assessing what has impacted you through the days will help you stay on top of your feelings. To prepare and prevent future setbacks, you can also create your crisis plan, which helps in mental health situations.

Develop a Personal Crisis Plan

Emergencies are more common than people care to talk about. By developing a personal crisis plan, you feel prepared with the resources you need to tackle troubles before they come up. You can draw up your crisis plan independently or involve your therapist and family in the process. Creating this plan is for you to maintain your peace of mind when faced with adversity. Everything you need in an emergency should be kept in a file, notebook, or folder accessible to you and other relevant people. Your crisis plan should include emergency numbers, medical information, steps to follow if you require professional assistance and multiple behaviors or emotions that may be concerning enough to count as an emergency. Medical information should account for all clinical contacts that could be needed, for example, your ER doctor, therapist contacts, and even your next of kin information. Also, include a list of diagnoses, medical history, medications you're taking, and so on. Essentially, your crisis plan covers everything that will be required from you during a tough time.

Build a Strong Support System

Having a crisis plan is essential, as is having people around you who can support you through setbacks. The healing journey can make you feel vulnerable and alone. Still, having a caring group of people to back you can empower you to overcome hardships. Your friends and family don't have to be the only people you turn to in times of trouble; you can also join a certified support group of people dealing with similar issues. During trauma recovery, having a group of people who have somewhat of an understanding of your sensitivities and feelings can offer a safe space to process your feelings. Interacting with groups of people on their healing journey can give you a chance to feel helpful to others, which can be a good break from dealing with your own emotions all the time. Support groups can be professionally led and organized by peers who want to create a healing environment for people with similar experiences.

Building a strong support system isn't always about talking about feelings. However, this is a great way to process them, and it can also involve doing fun activities. Go out and share experiences with people with similar interests and hobbies. A support system should comprise of people whose company you enjoy, and connecting with people through fun activities will feel refreshing. Interest-focused joint activities offer a time for you to pause from the heaviness of constantly addressing the feelings of ACEs. It's an opportunity to lift your spirits through movement. Hiking, bowling, and group walks are just a few examples of what you can do with your team of people as you navigate your healing. Maintaining momentum and progress in your journey is essential; in the next chapter, we'll explore why.

8

MAINTAINING PROGRESS—ENSURING SUSTAINABLE HEALING

Whatever you do, you have to keep moving forward.

— MARTIN LUTHER KING

It's easy to get so focused on the past during trauma healing that you forget to create effective strategies to heal and build a safe, empowering present and future. Tracking your signs of healing and your progress in the journey can help ease the overwhelming pressure of dealing with trauma-related issues. Maintaining progress requires you to constantly evaluate your triggers and how your traumas continue to impact you today. Experiencing ACEs or witnessing a traumatic event tends to have a negative, double-barreled ripple effect on your behaviors and emotions (Keelan, n.d.). First, the experience can cause intense and unpleasant feelings, creating negative thoughts and internal beliefs at the moment of the trauma and sometimes long after. Someone who has been sexually abused, for example, can feel emotions such as fear and shame. At the same time, thoughts like, "I'm worthless," 'I'm unsafe," and "People can't be trusted" can start to creep up. The second part of the ripple effect of an unfortunate event can be the personal belief that the situation left a wound that continues to interfere with daily life and could do so indefinitely. These two processes that happen from trauma are why it's important to continue tracking your progress. Noticing signs of healing can help you address the second element of the double-barreled effect of trauma by bringing you back to the present moment and helping you overcome re-traumatization. The more you learn your triggers, the less accurate the idea of trauma interfering with your present and future will be. Tracking your healing reduces the fallout or impact of your trauma over time.

TRACKING YOUR PROGRESS

Any form of progress begins with a goal, which is true in your healing journey. Recovering from PTSD and unwanted past events can be a lengthy journey, and it can be challenging for people to recognize their growth and improvement in the process. Likewise, some may lose themselves in the healing journey, not knowing what direction to take or how to monitor individual progress. Tracking your progress is a significant way to stay on top of your healing and continue on the path to self-empowerment and improvement. In the healing journey, self-evaluation is crucial because it helps you reflect on your goals to heal your inner child. Taking the time and making the effort to track your progress will help you take healing into your own hands. You will stay motivated to continue healing when you can track your progress. It will also give you insight into what you can improve for further recovery. Progress tracking is a nonlinear approach to trauma-informed care because it permits you to find effective and personal strategies to work through your trauma. Tracking your progress can happen in multiple ways, including mood-tracking, goal-setting, and paying attention to your habits. Understanding your daily processes can help improve your mental health and empower you from the wreck of past wounds.

Ways To Track Your Progress

To begin tracking your progress, come up with a list of ways that you would like to heal. Consider what you want to heal from, so think about your triggers, then make a list from there. For example, if you first think about how you were bullied or physically victimized during childhood, then write down how that negatively impacted you. It could have manifested through low self-esteem and viewing the world as threatening; if that's the case, then "having a positive view of myself" may be your goal for healing. As such, it should be listed as a sign of progress from your trauma. When you've done your list of goals for healing, you can use the following strategies to maintain momentum in your journey.

Journal

Write about your journey because this can be so healing. Also, seeing your goals on paper can help you actively work to achieve them. Chapter 2, healing and understanding your trauma, has laid a foundation for this information. A pen on paper is the old-school way to track your healing progress; you can write down points to help you identify how far you've come. Set a specific time of day when you can track your thoughts, feelings, activities, and any ideas that may arise during your process. Keeping a notebook is there to offer you a safe space where you can vent your emotions without judgment. When you feel overwhelmed or stuck, you can always return to your journal to inspire you on how far you've come. Remember to stay consistent in tracking your habits and patterns because that's how you'll make long-term changes. Studies suggest committing to developing new habits can lead to change within the first ten weeks of healing (Ede, 2023). Consistency can become positive automatic behaviors you'll start doing without thinking first.

Therapy Sessions

The healing journey is relentless; don't hesitate to walk the path with a psychologist or other therapist to help you track your progress. Therapy sessions are designed to help you process past events and find the most effective approach for your healing. Tracking your healing progress along with processing the events that have impacted you for so long should lead to a positive double-barreled effect during your therapy sessions. Most times, having external and professional input can help make your healing direction clearer. Therapy is a way to get someone trained to help you with your healing every step of the way, which beats doing it on your own.

Self-Reflection

Take the time to reflect on how far you've come regarding your list of healing goals. For example, in the case of learning to speak to yourself more kindly, consider how often you practice self-compassionate speaking in a day. Do you use self-affirming words? Are you redirecting your inner critic to focus on your strengths and the positive things about you? Though there's no linear way to measure your progress, reflecting on your goals and noting how often you work toward them through self-love practices can show you how deep you are in your healing journey.

Dealing With Feelings of Stagnation

The ups and downs in life are all evidence of the growth process. Sometimes in life, you will thrive and feel like you're meeting your expectations, but other times you won't. Stagnation occurs when you don't feel up to doing specific tasks, so your life stalls unexpectedly. The standstill can sometimes feel like something is actively holding you back from fulfilling your desires. Lack of connection and growth in life or your relationships can be an example of being stagnant. It is a period in your life where nothing excites or inspires you. Instead, you fall into a cycle of the mundane. Everyone gets in a rut from time to time; that's not something you should panic about. Instead, you need to focus your effort on working through it. Stagnation happens on a broad scale. Some examples of it in your daily life include lingering feelings of procrastination, lack of interest, or retreating into oversleeping and other idle activities. In many cases, being stagnant is evidence of underlying emotions and issues that can be identified through progress tracking.

To deal with feelings of stagnation, you need a goal-driven attitude that pushes you to make things happen rather than laying back and being a passive agent in your life. For example, keeping a journal or seeing a therapist is a way of remaining curious and active in your healing journey, which can help get you out of the rut you may be in. You can also have accountability partners to help you stay motivated throughout your journey. Your friends or family members are just the people who remind you of your goals and encourage you to keep going when stagnation threatens you. Getting out of a personal rut is about refusing to let fear and other strong emotions keep you stuck. Change your routine now and again to help you feel like you're adding some adventure to your life, and even challenge yourself to start new things. When you recognize you're stuck, accept what is, then allow yourself to create new habits that help you move away from that stagnation. Also, celebrating what you have can help get you out of the emotional rut.

Celebrating Small Victories

Your tracking process isn't just to identify what you can improve on but also to help you see what you have to celebrate. Lack of gratitude can keep you feeling like you aren't progressing in life, but celebrating your joys—even the tiniest of them—will empower you to accomplish bigger ones. When you celebrate the little things, it will boost your energy in the process. Keeping track of your progress also helps you see which victories you must celebrate. Anything you achieve in alignment with your goals should be celebrated, and it can be related to your personal healing, finances, work, and any other important aspect of your life. Celebrating the small wins pulls you away from harsh self-opinions and perfectionism, inspiring positive thinking and processing. Appreciation can help you turn your mistakes and shortcomings into successes by seeing adversity as growth rather than a dead end.

CONSISTENT PRACTICES FOR HEALING

Once you understand that you only have the moment you're in, it will make you better at being consistent in your healing. Consistency is key to healing childhood experiences that have found a way to impact your adulthood. Self-care practices, daily routines, and adjusting your healing plan can help you reach the mental health goals you want. Let's look at some of the practices you can commit to help foster healing.

The Role of Daily Routines in Sustaining Progress

Having a schedule is one of the easiest ways to provide yourself with consistency. Daily routines help your nervous system remain calm because you know exactly what the plan is for the day. Don't get me wrong; you can be flexible within your structures, schedules, and routines; there's no need for rigidity. If anything, you set a plan to put your mind at ease—even if it may change depending on the day. There's no all-or-nothing thinking when it comes to creating a consistent schedule. Even with unexpected occurrences, knowing how to start and end your day will put you at ease for it. Inconsistent scheduling, on the other hand, may increase the state of nervousness you feel in your body. Your nervous system can go into overdrive trying to solve the uncontrollable stuff, especially when you don't have a set plan for how to go about each day. Establishing a set routine can be considered a trauma-informed approach to healing, one which helps you improve your emotional well-being. It's also a form of caring for yourself.

Balancing Self-Care Practice

Self-care can breathe a moment of peace, giving you a break from survival mode. Initially, self-care can seem challenging to do, especially when you try new things. But it's a way to encourage your growth and increase your sense of self-confidence. After all the heartache you've been through, you deserve to live a little and take some time to nourish yourself. In Chapter 4, we address self-love and care and how valuable it is for you to take ownership of your needs across all aspects of your being. Balancing self-care practice with everything you've learned in this chapter will expand your capacity to move from survival to thriving.

Adjust Your Practices as Your Healing Evolves

Whatever routines and self-care practices you decide to do for yourself, remember to stay flexible enough to permit yourself to readjust when things are no longer working. No fixed timeline exists for when you should fully heal from ACEs or other trauma. Part of maintaining progress is giving yourself the grace to navigate your process as gradually as possible. Remove the self-imposed pressure of having to bounce back from setbacks as quickly as the world expects you to. Adjusting your practices is a way of honoring your healing on your own time and taking the necessary steps to ensure that you do it effectively. Healing isn't straightforward; it may be as complex as the trauma itself, so take your time. Recognize that some methods may only work for a short while before you need to change them, and when that happens, allow yourself the courtesy of transformation. It's all a massive part of your healing process, so be intentional but go slowly toward your goals. Also, keep people around you who will support you as you heal.

BUILDING A SUPPORTIVE COMMUNITY

Having supportive communities is vital in facilitating your healing and helping you maintain your progress. The support in your life can act as accountability partners who cheer you on and lift you up through your journey. When you have valuable people in your life, it can also prevent you from doing things from a place of shame and help you to see your worth in many ways. Community is a comfort to our souls and hearts; that's an important part of your healing journey. Church groups, book clubs, sports teams, activity buddies, and even online support groups on Facebook or WhatsApp are examples of multiple communities. People who attend AA-type groups are also a part of an understanding and supportive community of individuals who are integral to their healing.

Even Ibrahim realizes the value that tapping into spiritual healing can have on growing in community with others, "As humans, if we cannot connect with the full intensity that is the essence of the web of life all around us, then we feel weak and victimized" (Kurdieh, 2019). Everyone's road to spiritual connection is different; whether you're an atheist, Christian, Buddhist, or nonconforming, your journey has a purpose and can promote healing. It's even better when you can get into a community of people who share the same understanding as you do in this area. The objective is to join a community of people where you can hold each other accountable for the steps required for healing. In these groups, mutual support and respect are facilitated to encourage each person to be true to their journey. It's essential to not only receive help but also offer support to others. Support groups are imperative for everyone on the path to healing because they are a way to build community, which will nurture your growth and wellness. When you have a safe space and secure people to turn to, you'll feel even more courageous to take on new things and grow as an individual. It will set the scene for you to thrive in your life after trauma, an idea that will be explored in the following chapter.

9

THRIVING AFTER TRAUMA— CULTIVATING A LIFE OF JOY AND FULFILLMENT

Healing requires us to stop struggling and to enjoy life more and endure it less.

— DARINA STOYANOVA

Learning to celebrate personal growth is imperative in the healing journey. Post-traumatic growth (PTG) is a topic in positive psychology that values the possibility of thriving after trauma. Developed by Richard Tedeschi and Lawrence Calhoun, PTG is a transformation-based theory acknowledging that positive change can happen after traumatic events. Even though you've been hurt, you can still have a fruitful and empowering life. This chapter concerns recognizing your growth, working toward PTG, and forging your way to fulfillment. A successful personal growth journey happens when you stay motivated to improve and strive to make meaningful changes. Progress is a cornerstone of cultivating a life of joy and fulfillment; this journey has nothing to do with being perfect or not making any mistakes. You're succeeding as long as you are here, still showing your willingness to learn, adapt, and grow.

RECOGNIZING PERSONAL GROWTH

This is your moment; please take the time to reflect on all the work you've had to do through each chapter. Recognizing and celebrating personal growth during your healing experience will continue your transformation. Personal growth is more about improving and walking the journey than it is about reaching some sort of destination. Self-growth and self-improvement are synonyms of personal growth, both of which honor the sentiment that growth is a continuous process, and so is your healing. Learn to take the time you need daily to be kinder to yourself as you go through these processes. Healing and growing are about planning to improve your habits, behaviors, responses, choices, and actions in alignment with your envisioned best self. Once you've established a plan of multiple healing goals, you can start working toward your personal growth. For you to have gotten this far shows that you've already begun your processes, and your progress is something to behold. Examples of personal growth include reaching milestones, big or small, that you've set for yourself. You've grown if you battled with anger emotionally and learned new ways to manage it better. Learning how to overcome procrastination, facing your fears, becoming more responsible, and adopting a more optimistic outlook on life are all valuable examples of individual growth. This list shows you that growing doesn't need to be visible to other people; if anything, the most incredible growth processes happen internally. The mere willingness to step out of what's familiar so you can learn anew is a powerful trait of a growing person. Doing uncomfortable things in an attempt to become better for yourself and others is good for you.

Growth is when you keep pushing despite adversity; it's knowing that you can always be better than you were yesterday and then taking the steps to get there. That's how resilience is built and maintained. With that said, take more than a second to acknowledge and honor the strength you've gained through the healing journey. Your resilience and healing are both processes that require you to continue on the path of self-discovery and adaptability through every life experience. Give yourself compassion in knowing how far you've come. Even with your wounds, you haven't allowed past traumas to keep you stuck. Instead, you've bought a journal, started healing practices, picked up a self-help book, and begun to reclaim your story; you should be proud of yourself.

POST-TRAUMATIC GROWTH

Speaking of growth, PTSD can play with the psyche to convince us that we can't thrive once we've been affected by trauma, but nothing is more untrue. PTG is possible for every single one of us, yourself included! Though closely linked to resilience, PTG is unique in that it acknowledges the difficulties in bouncing back from setbacks. The growth that occurs after trauma is complex and riddled with profound challenges and changes to one's view of the world. People who go through PTG must battle their core beliefs and endure psychological hardships before finding personal growth on the other side. Yet, resilience is the personal ability to overcome, and it has less focus on the deep inner work that needs to be achieved before one can be labeled victorious. Individual growth after trauma is a process that takes a lot of effort, time, wrestling, and energy. Someone resilient isn't necessarily shaken to the core when confronted by hardships, compared to someone who experiences PTG. Traumatic event survivors often need to adopt new beliefs that go against how they may want to feel in response to their trauma. Someone a parent has abused may be justified in resenting their caregiver and having difficulties trusting authority. Still, PTG seeks to reframe this outlook entirely. The hope is to reach a place of forgiveness that allows people to overcome resentment and use their personal trauma to become better parents. Allowing yourself to grow beyond trauma will help deepen your connections with people and increase your empathy and emotional strength. PTG is probably one of the most challenging yet rewarding paths to take. It can lead to long-lasting resilience and fulfillment.

CREATING A FULFILLING LIFE AFTER TRAUMA

Having an appreciation for your life after trauma is one of five areas associated with PTG. The simple fact that you've survived traumatic events proves there's still so much more left for you to pursue and accomplish. You got a second, third, fourth, and fifth chance because your story isn't supposed to end yet. You're meant to use your trauma to show yourself and others that it can be overcome. Creating a fulfilling life after trauma requires you to have a positive outlook on the life you now have. Sure, it may look different, but it's yours, and you get to rebuild and redesign it how you want. The second area that needs to be satisfied in PTG is your relationships with others. Give yourself the chance to reestablish trust with people and foster positive, strong connections.

Living the rest of your life in isolation stops you from reaching your full potential. If you aim to grow, you need to find a safe and comfortable way to let people into your life again. You'll be surprised how many people want to see you thrive and help you get there. Being open to new possibilities after trauma is the third aspect of PTG. Don't let negative experiences rob you of your future. Traumatic situations have already taken too many days of your life just by you reliving them in your mind. You have to do everything you can to prevent them from taking the hope for a bright future because there is hope for you yet. The refusal to back down and the resilience you show in the face of adversity will bring up the fourth aspect of PTG: Personal strength. Once you've decided to push through the pain by accepting and releasing what you've experienced, you'll reach a level of power that you can't even imagine having post-trauma. Lastly, you'll experience the fifth and final aspect of your transformation, which is spiritual. The change you go through during PTG helps facilitate a thriving life after trauma, and you deserve every single positive result. Here are a few things you can focus on in your journey to healing and fulfillment after trauma.

Pursue Your Passions

Even after trauma, you can regain your passions and create positivity. You are finding joy in activities you enjoyed before negative experiences can bring back the light snuffed away during the situation. You'll also find that, sometimes, trauma makes it hard to return to what you used to love. Perhaps, through PTG, you'll find that you have new interests—and that's okay. Meet yourself where you are and pursue the passions that you have today. Think of pursuing your passions as a decision to revive your life's purpose; discover new activities and hobbies to reignite the spark you had before the trauma. Join a chess club or sign up for water sports, whatever your heart desires. Go into your life and start doing things to show yourself that you aren't just surviving and living. Your passion and positivity can also be rekindled by the compassion and connection you foster with others.

Keep Building Relationships and Resilience

When you feel connected to people, you become more prone to building trust with them. Increased security and trust in personal bonds are linked to oxytocin. This hormone enhances pro-social behavior and promotes a feeling of safety. It can significantly reduce unwanted, intense feelings of stress, fear, and anxiety, which inevitably contribute to building your resilience. Your story is just beginning, so continue fostering healthy habits and restoring positive connections.

Appreciate Your Inner Strength

The trauma you've experienced may not be something you would have chosen for yourself, but it has proved your strength. Learn to appreciate the personal toughness that trauma has revealed to you. Maybe you never thought you'd survive anything as painful as the experience you've been through, yet you did just that. Through the agony, you somehow channeled your inner strength and found a way to stand again. Your inner strength isn't something to undermine but to be appreciated. Not only did you get through the adversity, but you've found a way to build a new life after it. The distance you've created between where you were then and where you are now is commendable. It's a huge achievement, so celebrate it. Appreciate yourself every day that you choose to face your aches rather than hide or run from them. Acknowledging your strength and how far you've come is not prideful or arrogant; it's honorable and justified. You are a remarkable person, childhood trauma and all, and you should celebrate every ounce of who you've grown and are growing to be.

Most survivors of childhood trauma tend to personalize the experience. Ibrahim did, and it's okay if you battle with this, too. Questions like "Why me?" and "What did I do to deserve this?" can overwhelm the mind of a survivor (Kurdieh, 2019). While it isn't your fault, and you never deserved that harmful experience, being told that doesn't always feel empowering. Your suffering isn't meaningless because you are someone of value, so instinctively, everything that you encounter changes to match your purpose. Your suffering and past hurt have happened to reveal the reason you are here, a revelation Ibrahim describes as "your soul's purpose." It's through understanding your trauma and channeling power through it that you can truly live out its meaning. Trauma only disempowers you when you dwell in it rather than use it as a source of empowerment. The process of overcoming childhood hurt and uncovering hidden pain is the healing journey, and it is also the path you should follow to become the best version of yourself possible.

CONCLUSION

Purpose, motivation, joy, and restoration will find you as you walk in love, community, and truth. Overcoming childhood adversity can make you feel like you can get through anything. Feeling empowered to live your truth and tell your story makes it possible to find support and strengthen your connections with people. Trauma wants you to run and hide in shame, but confronting it makes you realize you have nothing to feel ashamed of. Your experiences are meant to pass through you on your way to personal growth and self-discovery. Lift your wounds to the light so they can heal, and you can come out of hiding. You'll notice a shift in your mindset through therapy and internal acknowledgment over time. You will become empowered to the point where stories of your past and describing your experiences will not make you feel like cringing, physically and emotionally. Don't quit on yourself; your healing creates a safe space to hold your head high as you re-cultivate self-confidence and happiness.

Quite frankly, it takes time to get there. After all these years, I'm also still working through my healing process of overcoming childhood trauma. Part of the reason for wanting to write this book is to make my path toward healing. The other part is to reveal what's hidden beneath the surface; just as I was surprised about my personal trauma but found a way to recognize it, I want to help you come to the same realization. Examining your past will give you the blueprint for your best future. Recently, I've been listening to or working on many things that point to the idea of healing and moving forward being an internal job before anything else. To overcome this, you must look to the past for insight and perspective to move forward with a clearer path and purpose. Though looking back can be daunting because the past is often full of hurt and disappointment, that is precisely where you'll find your perspective and meaning. Maybe the issues you are currently dealing with might come from childhood trauma that still needs to be addressed, and the steps in this book help you do that. So don't be afraid to examine your past because your best future depends on it.

Keep working through trauma until your heart overflows with joy from reading your survival story. Be patient and compassionate with yourself as you recognize your pains and heal from them. The process may be slow, but progress is happening, and you need to trust that. The crucial part of your journey is owning your entire story, even the parts you wouldn't have wanted to experience. The most significant benefit of confronting your trauma with gentle intention is that you begin to make sense of what once seemed so senseless. Healing from ACEs initially feels overwhelming, but you have support and many options to see you through. Learn to lean on your community and the people who are open to talking things out with you. Also, embrace new activities to help you fall in love with your life again. You can start to rebuild, reframe, and restore positive meaning in everything you do from today onward. Not many people have the courage to face the wounds of childhood and improve their adult lives due to it. You, however, are finding your way through the most unpleasant memories and confrontations. Using the information and strategies from the book, you can become living proof of a fulfilling life after hard experiences. PTSD can be transformed into PTG with enough effort and willingness to put in the inner work. You are the narrator of your story, so you can change and influence it however you desire—even when bad things happen that you have no control over. You have the final say, not trauma; remember this as you continue in your journey to healing. I wish you the best on your path from pain to power and purpose.

LEAVE A REVIEW!

★★★★

I hope you found it resonating as you've navigated the "How to Overcome Childhood Trauma" pages. Reflecting on the words of Maya Angelou: "There is no greater agony than bearing an untold story inside you." Your story, your experience with this book, is a part of that tale.

Your thoughts are pure gold. Sharing them not only spreads wisdom, helping others glean insights before even opening the first page, but it also acts as a signpost for someone at a crossroads. Moreover, every review boosts the message, increasing its visibility and amplifying its potential to change lives.

So, would you drop a line or two? By scanning the QR code and sharing your thoughts, you become a beacon for many seeking guidance. Thank you for being part of this journey.

GLOSSARY

Adverse Childhood Experiences (ACEs): Any potentially traumatic ordeal that happens during childhood.

Cognitive Behavioral Therapy (CBT): A form of psychotherapy that helps people understand the thoughts and feelings that influence their behaviors.

Dissociation: A psychological experience of feeling disconnected from one's sensory experience, sense of self, or personal history.

Eye Movement Desensitization and Reprocessing (EMDR): A type of psychotherapy that targets symptoms of trauma and emotional distress to promote healing.

Flashbacks: Sudden, vivid, and often unpleasant memories of past events.

Grounding: Techniques used to inspire a sense of presence and away from traumatic memories or dissociative states.

Healing Journey: The ongoing process of overcoming trauma

Inner Child: A term to describe an individual's child-like aspect.

Post-Traumatic Stress Disorder (PTSD): A psychiatric condition that can develop in people who have experienced or witnessed traumatic situations.

Post-Traumatic Growth (PTG): The transformation that occurs after battling wounds caused by traumatic encounters.

Resilience: The ability to adapt and recover from stress, adversity, trauma, or tragedy.

Safe Space: An environment in which a person or group of people can feel confident and protected from discrimination, criticism, harassment, or any other emotional or physical harm.

Survivor: A term used to describe the strength and resilience of people who overcome trauma.

Trauma-Informed Care: A framework used to recognize, understand, and address the effects of all types of trauma.

Triggers: Any reminder of a traumatic event that sets off an overwhelming reaction.

Validation: Acknowledgment and acceptance of personal experiences and emotions.

REFERENCES

Ackerman, C. (2018, December 22). *What is self-image in psychology? How do we improve it?* Positive Psychology/ https://positivepsychology.com/self-image/

American Psychological Association. (n.d.). *Resilience.* APA. https://www.apa.org/topics/resilience

Anchor Therapy. (2021, October 6). *How to heal childhood trauma as an adult.* Blog. https://www.anchortherapy.org/blog/how-to-heal-childhood-trauma-as-an-adult

Ann, J. (2021, March 5). *It didn't start with you: How inherited family trauma shapes who we are and how to end the cycle by Mark Wolynn.* Medium: A Book Review. https://medium.com/crescent-moon/it-didnt-start-with-you-how-inherited-family-trauma-shapes-who-we-are-and-how-to-end-the-cycle-by-307f3227066d

APA Dictionary of Psychology. (n.d.). *Resilience.* Psychology Topics. https://www.apa.org/topics/resilience

Arzt, N. (2022, October 17). *Attachment disorders in adults: Types, symptoms, & symptoms.* Choosing Therapy. https://www.choosingtherapy.com/attachment-disorders-adults/

Barkley, S. (2023, May 3). *17 Inspiring quotes about setting healthy boundaries.* PsychCentral. https://psychcentral.com/health/quotes-healthy-boundaries

Blog Admin. (2021, January 11). *Your relationships are a reflection of you.* Pyramid Valley International, Bengaluru. https://www.pyramidvalley.org/post/radiant-relationships

Botwin, S. (2021, December 18). *Moving safely through PTSD recovery.* Psychology Today. https://www.psychologytoday.com/za/blog/thriving-after-trauma/202112/moving-safely-through-ptsd-recovery

Boyes, A. (2021, December 28). *Are you feeling stagnant? Here's what to try.* Psychology Today. https://www.psychologytoday.com/intl/blog/in-practice/202112/are-you-feeling-stagnant-heres-what-try

Brandt, A. (2018, April 2). *9 Steps to healing childhood trauma as an adult.* Psychology Today. https://www.psychologytoday.com/za/blog/mindful-anger/201804/9-steps-healing-childhood-trauma-adult

Brickel, R. E. (2015, July 29). *Trauma-informed care: Understanding the many challenges of toxic stress.* Brixkel & Associates. https://brickelandassociates.com/trauma-informed-care-understanding-the-pervasive-challenges-of-toxic-stres/

Brickel, R. E. (n.d.). *To heal trauma, free your most compassionate self.* PsychAlive. https://www.psychalive.org/heal-trauma-free-compassionate-self/

128 | REFERENCES

Brook. (n.d.). *Setting boundaries: Cassie's story*. Relationships. https://www.brook.org.uk/your-life/setting-boundaries-cassies-story/

CaringBridge Staff. (2023, October 2). *How to build a strong support system*. Helping. https://www.caringbridge.org/resources/how-to-build-a-strong-support-system/

Casabianca, S. S. (2022, October 28). *7 Signs someone doesn't respect your boundaries and what to do*. PsychCentral. https://psychcentral.com/relationships/signs-boundary-violations#being-on-repeat

Cherry, K. (n.d.). *Introspection and how it is used in psychology research*. Verywellmind. https://www.verywellmind.com/what-is-introspection-2795252

Cherry, K. (n.d.). *How resilience helps you cope with life's challenges*. Verywellmind. https://www.verywellmind.com/what-is-resilience-2795059

Children's Center. (n.d.). *Breaking the silence*. Survivor Stories. https://www.childrens-center.org/survivor-stories/

Cikanavicius, D. (2018, May 14). *5 Ways childhood neglect and trauma skews our self-esteem*. PsychCentral. https://psychcentral.com/blog/psychology-self/2018/05/childhood-self-esteem#2

Cleveland Clinic. (n.d.). *Fostering a positive self-image*. https://my.clevelandclinic.org/health/articles/12942-fostering-a-positive-self-image

Collier, L. (2016). Growth after trauma. *Monitor on Psychology*, 47(10), 1–48. https://www.apa.org/monitor/2016/11/growth-trauma

Cooks-Campbell, A. (2022, May 26). *What self-love truly means and ways to cultivate it*. BetterUp. https://www.betterup.com/blog/self-love

Cooks-Campbell, A. (2022, July 15). *Triggered? Learn how to recognize the feeling and keep it in check*. BetterUp. https://www.betterup.com/blog/triggers

Covington, C. (2018, September 17). *How adult survivors of childhood trauma forge their own paths to recovery*. Texas Standard. https://www.texasstandard.org/stories/how-adult-survivors-of-childhood-trauma-forge-their-own-paths-to-recovery/

Davis, S. (2022, May 16). *Trauma, stress, and resilience*. Complex PTSD Healing. https://cptsdfoundation.org/2022/05/16/trauma-stress-and-resilience/

Denver Metro Counselling. (n.d.). *3 Ways a consistent schedule can help trauma*. Trauma. https://denvermetrocounseling.com/3-ways-a-consistent-schedule-can-help-trauma/

Ede, R. (2023, April 12). *8 Habits tracking apps for boosting your well-being in 2023*. Forbes Health. https://www.forbes.com/health/mind/best-habit-tracking-apps/

Eatough, E. (2023, May 17). *15 red flags in a relationship to look out for*. BetterUp. https://www.betterup.com/blog/red-flags-in-a-relationship

Elmer, J. (2021, August 20). *Creating a mental health crisis plan*. PsychCentral. https://psychcentral.com/health/creating-a-mental-health-crisis-plan

Fisher, J. (2017). Healing the fragmented selves of trauma survivors: Overcoming internal self-alienation. *Routledge*. 1-280.

Foundation Title. (n.d.). *Fostering and maintaining strong relationships*. https://ftnj.com/fostering-and-maintaining-strong-relationships/

FSR Editor. (n.d.). *How can progress tracking improve my recovery experience?* First Steps Recovery. https://firststepsrecovery.com/how-can-progress-tracking-improve-my-recovery-experience/

Ghekiere, E. (2018, March 23). *20+ Positive self image quotes to boost anyone's confidence.* Page Flutter. https://pageflutter.com/20-positive-self-image-quotes/

Garrett, C. (2022, April 23). *Overcoming setbacks and challenges.* Medium. https://medium.com/change-your-mind/overcoming-setbacks-and-challenges-f46fb404fb59

Gigante, V. (n.d.). *7 Tips to develop a daily practice for growth, healing, and happiness.* Tint Buddha. https://tinybuddha.com/blog/7-tips-to-develop-a-daily-practice-for-growth-healing-and-happiness/

Gildersleeve, J. (2014). Wound: The hotel and to the north. In Elizabeth Bowen and the Writing of Trauma. *Leiden, The Netherlands: Brill.* https://doi.org/10.1163/9789401210478_003

Gillihan, S. J. (2019, March 6). *The healing power of telling your trauma story.* Psychology Today. https://www.psychologytoday.com/intl/blog/think-act-be/201903/the-healing-power-telling-your-trauma-story

Grande, D. (2021, October 27). *Defense mechanisms: Definition, types, & examples.* Choosing Therapy. https://www.choosingtherapy.com/defense-mechanisms/

Guest Author. (2021, June 25). *Moving on: the effect of stagnation on your mental health and wellbeing.* RTOR.org. https://www.rtor.org/2021/06/25/moving-on-the-effect-of-stagnation-on-your-mental-health-and-wellbeing/

Gupta, S. (n.d.). *What is trauma therapy?* Verwellmind. https://www.verywellmind.com/trauma-therapy-definition-types-techniques-and-efficacy-5191413

Harris, R. (2021, June 21). *ACT Tips: The "Four As" of Acceptance.* Psychwire. https://psychwire.com/harris/blog/1radzhw/act-tips-the-four-as-of-acceptance

Harvard Health Publishing. (2010, December 1). *The health benefits of strong relationships.* Staying Healthy. https://www.health.harvard.edu/staying-healthy/the-health-benefits-of-strong-relationships

Healey, J. (2021, March 2). *11 Powerful quotes about healing from trauma.* Healing Brave. https://healingbrave.com/blogs/all/quotes-about-healing-from-trauma

HelpGuide.org. (n.d.). *Emotional and psychological trauma.* PTSD & Trauma.

https://www.helpguide.org/articles/ptsd-trauma/coping-with-emotional-and-psychological-trauma.htm

Henden, J. (2020). A broad overview of solution focused severe trauma & stress recovery work, with the introduction of two additional SF recovery work, with the introduction of two Additional SF Instruments to promote thriverhood instruments to promote thriverhood. *Journal of Solution Focused Practices,* 4(2). https://digitalscholarship.unlv.edu/cgi/viewcontent.cgi?article=1080&context=journalsfp

Ho, L. (2023, February 3). *How to celebrate small wins to achieve big goals.* Life Hack. https://www.lifehack.org/396379/how-celebrate-small-wins-achieve-big-goals

Holland, K. (2020, June 27). *Positive self-talk: Talking to yourself is a good thing.* Healthline. https://www.healthline.com/health/positive-self-talk#examples-of-positive-self--talk

Hopeful Panda. (2023, February 28). *18 Ways to build more resilience after childhood trauma.* Coping Methods. https://hopefulpanda.com/how-to-build-resilience/

International Society for Traumatic Stress Studies (ISTSS). (n.d.). *Trauma and relationships.* ISTSS. https://istss.org/ISTSS_Main/media/Documents/ISTSS_TraumaAndRelationships_FNL.pdf

Jones, R. (2022, November 24). *75 Childhood trauma quotes to get past your trauma.* Happier Human. https://www.happierhuman.com/childhood-trauma-quotes/

Jordan, B. (n.d.). *Good communication skills: open-ended questions.* About Leaders. https://aboutleaders.com/good-communication-skills-open-ended-questions/

Kaplan, E. (n.d.). *7 Tips for overcoming setbacks.* Medium. https://medium.com/@ellekaplan/7-tips-for-overcoming-setbacks-c532eb4d462a

Keelan, P. (n.d). *The importance of tracking signs of healing from a traumatic event.* PK Registered Psychologist. https://drpatrickkeelan.com/anxiety/the-importance-of-tracking-signs-of-healing-from-a-traumatic-event/

King-White, D. (2022, June 7). *Childhood trauma: Types, causes, signs, and treatments.* Choosing Therapy. https://www.choosingtherapy.com/childhood-trauma/

Kohrt, B. A., Ottman, K., Panter-Brick, C., Konner, M., & Patel, V. (2020). Why we heal: The evolution of psychological healing and implications for global mental health. *Clinical Psychology Review, 82,* 101920. https://doi.org/10.1016/j.cpr.2020.101920

Kuhlmann, M. (2019, January 31). *The reality of setbacks.* Blog. https://www.michaelkuhlmann.com/76874/the-reality-of-setbacks/

Kurdieh, I. (2019, November 22). *How I overcame my childhood trauma.* Medium.

https://medium.com/@internalworlds/how-i-overcame-my-childhood-trauma-f44eb81fed36

Laffey, L. K. (2017, November 14). *How to regain passion and positivity after trauma.* Trauma Therapy. https://lindaklaffey.com/how-to-regain-passion-and-positivity-after-trauma/

Lahousen, T., Unterrainer, H. F., & Kapfhammer, P. (2019). Psychobiology of Attachment and Trauma—Some General Remarks From a Clinical Perspective. *Frontiers in Psychiatry, 10.* https://doi.org/10.3389/fpsyt.2019.00914

Lebow, H. (2023, January 21). *How does your body remember trauma?* PsychCentral. https://psychcentral.com/health/how-your-body-remembers-trauma

Li, P. (2023, June 26). *Childhood emotional neglect–37 Signs, effects and how to overcome.* Parenting for Brain. https://www.parentingforbrain.com/childhood-emotional-neglect/

Linney, S. (n.d.). *Letting go of shame.* American Addiction Centers. https://americanaddictioncenters.org/blog/acceptance-is-part-of-recovery

Lonczak, H. S. (2020, July 24). *Increase clients' self-love: 26 Exercises & worksheets.* Positive Psychology. https://positivepsychology.com/self-love-exercises-worksheets/

Mackey, M. (2023, May 6). *100 Quotes about self-care, because being good to yourself has never been more important.* Parade. https://parade.com/1070248/maureenmackey/self-care-quotes/

Mager, D. (2016, February 8). *Trauma tips for understanding and healing–Part 1 of 4.* Psychology Today. https://www.psychologytoday.com/intl/blog/some-assembly-required/201602/trauma-tips-understanding-and-healing-part-1-4

Maidenberg. M. (2022, March 3). *The healing power of radical acceptance.* Psychology Today. https://www.psychologytoday.com/za/blog/being-your-best-self/202203/the-healing-power-radical-acceptance

Mandroita, M. (2021, October 13). *Here is how to identify your attachment style.* PsychCentral. https://psychcentral.com/health/4-attachment-styles-in-relationships#disorganized-attachment

Mayo Clinic Staff. (2022, October 11). *Consumer health.* Mayo Clinic. https://www.mayoclinic.org/healthy-lifestyle/consumer-health/in-depth/mindfulness-exercises/art-20046356

Mayo Clinic Staff. (2022, July 6). *Adult health.* Mayo Clinic. https://www.mayoclinic.org/healthy-lifestyle/adult-health/in-depth/self-esteem/art-20045374

McAulay, L. (2020, August 11). *8 Ways to embrace self-love and thank your body.* https://www.healthline.com/health/8-ways-to-embrace-self-love-and-thank-your-body

McDonald, J. N. (2023, June 6). *36 Healing quotes for inspiration and encouragement.* Southern Living. https://www.southernliving.com/culture/healing-quotes

Meah, A. (2023). *35 Inspirational quotes on progress.* Awaken the Greatness Within. https://www.awakenthegreatnesswithin.com/35-inspirational-quotes-on-progress/

Mental Health Connection. (n.d.). *Statistics.* http://recognizetrauma.org/statistics.php

Michigan ACE Initiative. (2019, October 1). *How to recognize if your childhood trauma is affecting you as an adult (& How to heal).* Blog. https://www.miace.org/2019/10/01/how-to-recognize-if-your-childhood-trauma-is-affecting-you-as-an-adult-how-to-heal/

Millacci, T. (2017, February 28). *What is gratitude and why is it so important?* Positive Psychology. https://positivepsychology.com/gratitude-appreciation/

Morin, A. (2023, July 27). *Understanding the effects of childhood trauma.* Verywellmind. https://www.verywellmind.com/what-are-the-effects-of-childhood-trauma-4147640

Nash, J. (2018, January 5). *How to set healthy boundaries & build positive relationships.* Positive Psychology. https://positivepsychology.com/great-self-care-setting-healthy-boundaries/

Nash, J. (n.d.). *Dealing with boundary violations.* Positive Psychology. https://positive.b-cdn.net/wp-content/uploads/2022/11/Dealing-With-Boundary-Violations.pdf

Neff, K. (n.d.). *Self-compassion.* The Center for Mindful Self-Compassion. https://self-compassion.org/

Nickerson, C. (2023, February 13). *What is self-image and how do we improve it?* Simply Psychology. https://www.simplypsychology.org/self-image.html

Northstar Transitions. (2021, January 5). *How to monitor your progress in recovery.* https://www.northstartransitions.com/post/how-to-monitor-your-progress-in-recovery

Nunez, K. (2020, September 10). *The benefits of guided imagery and how to do it.* Healthline. https://www.healthline.com/health/guided-imagery

Orentas, G. (2021, August 2). *Signs and symptoms of PTSD in women.* PsychCentral. https://psychcentral.com/ptsd/signs-and-symptoms-of-ptsd-in-women

Pattemore, C. (2021, June 3). *10 Ways to build and preserve better boundaries.* PsychCentral. https://psychcentral.com/lib/10-way-to-build-and-preserve-better-boundaries#10-tips

Positive Thinking Mind. (n.d.). *9 Simple tips to focus on what you can control.* Personal Growth. https://positivethinkingmind.com/focus-on-what-you-can-control/

Psychology Today Staff. (n.d.). *Relationships center.* Psychology Today. https://www.psychologytoday.com/us/basics/relationships

Quotlr. (n.d.). *Cheering interpersonal relationship quotations.*Interpersonal Relationship Quotes. https://quotlr.com/quotes-about-interpersonal-relationship

Resnick, A. (2023, February 18). *How to heal from trauma.* Verywellmind. https://www.verywellmind.com/10-ways-to-heal-from-trauma-5206940

Robinson, L., Smith, M., & Segal, J. (n.d.). *Emotional and psychological trauma.* PTSD & Trauma: Help Guide. https://www.helpguide.org/articles/ptsd-trauma/coping-with-emotional-and-psychological-trauma.htm

Roncero, A. (2021, December 29). *Childhood trauma: 3 steps to start healing.* BetterUp. https://www.betterup.com/blog/childhood-trauma

Ryder, G. (2022, January 19). *What is attachment trauma.* PsychCentral. https://psychcentral.com/health/attachment-trauma

Quinn, M., Caldara, G., Collins, K., Owens, H., Ifeoma, O., Loudermilk, E., & Stinson, J. D. (2018). Methods for understanding childhood trauma: Modifying the adverse childhood experiences international questionnaire for cultural competency. *Int J Public Health* 63, 149–151. https://doi.org/10.1007/s00038-017-1058-2

Sasson, R. (n.d.). *What is personal growth and why you need it.* Success Consciousness. https://www.successconsciousness.com/blog/personal-development/what-is-personal-growth/

Scala, V. (2021, October 6). *How to heal childhood trauma as an adult.* Anchor Therapy. https://www.anchortherapy.org/blog/how-to-heal-childhood-trauma-as-an-adult

Scott, E. (2022, October 19). *18 Effective stress relief strategies.* Verywellmind. https://www.verywellmind.com/tips-to-reduce-stress-3145195

Shafir, H. (2022, July 29). *15 Signs of repressed childhood trauma in adults.* Choosing Therapy. https://www.choosingtherapy.com/signs-of-repressed-childhood-trauma-in-adults/

Smith, M., Robinson, L., & Segal, J. (n.d.). *The emotional response to traumatic events.* Help Guide. https://www.helpguide.org/articles/ptsd-trauma/traumatic-stress.htm

Swaim, E. (2022, May 25). *7 Reminders to carry with you on your trauma recovery journey.* Healthline. https://www.healthline.com/health/mental-health/trauma-recovery

Teach Trauma. (n.d.). *Trauma's impact on attachment.* Information About Trauma. https://teachtrauma.com/information-about-trauma/traumas-impact-on-attachment/

The Happiness Doctor. (2020, January 1). *7 Ways to heal your old emotional wounds.* Inner Child Healing. https://www.thehappinessdoctor.com/blog/7-ways-to-heal-your-old-emotional-wounds

The Village Family Service Center. (2023, July 17). *Tips for adapting after trauma and stress*. The Village Blog. https://www.thevillagefamily.org/blog/tips-adapting-after-trauma-and-stress

Workplace Resilience and Wellbeing. (n.d.). *Mastering resilience: Strong relationships toolkit*. Wraw. https://thewellbeingproject.co.uk/wp-content/uploads/2021/12/Wraw-Strong-Relationships-Toolkit-print.pdf

Yang, B. (2022, November 18). *Awakening with Brian*. [Instagram Reel]. https://www.instagram.com/reel/ClFMD7zPlsS/?igshid=ODk2MDJkZDc2Zg%3D%3D

Printed in Great Britain
by Amazon